No Experience Necessary

Unit Two: You're Hired

Kelly A. Fryer
Rolf A. Jacobson

No Experience Necessary
Bible Study
Unit Two: You're Hired

Copyright © 2005
Augsburg Fortress. All
rights reserved. Except
for brief quotations in
critical articles or reviews,
no part of this book
may be reproduced in
any manner without prior
written permission from
the publisher. Write to:
Permissions, Augsburg
Fortress, Box 1209,
Minneapolis, MN 55440.

Editors:
Gloria E. Bengtson
Laurie J. Hanson
Eileen K. Zahn

Series logo, cover,
and interior design:
Marti Naughton

Cover and interior
images:
BananaStock
Brand X Pictures
Comstock
Digital Vision Inc.
Dover Publications
Dreamstime.com
Eyewire
Ingram Publishing
Photodisc
Pueblo Publishing
   Company Inc.

ISBN 0-8066-4811-2
Manufactured in U.S.A.

1 2 3 4 5 6 7 8 9 0 1 2 3 4 5 6 7 8 9

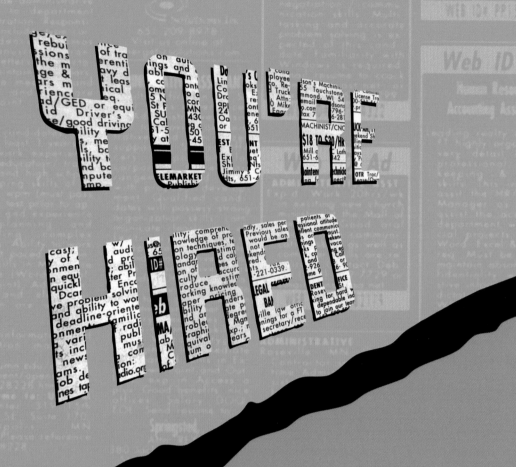

INTRODUCTION

SESSIONS

Everybody's welcome!

Welcome to the No Experience Necessary Bible study series! It doesn't matter if this is your first or 101st Bible study. No Experience Necessary is designed to be accessible for people new to Bible study and full of fresh insights for others.

Everybody's welcome. No roadblocks. No jargon. No experience necessary.

God's speaking.

Right here. Right now. That's the radically simple assumption at the heart of this Bible study. What's God saying to you? What's God saying to us?

Come as you are.

You can read. You've got common sense. You've got your own experiences. Well, here's the Bible. Off you go. Anyone can be a facilitator for this Bible study too. No special knowledge needed.

You decide.

Many Bible studies tell you what to do. Not this one. No Experience Necessary starts with you. What you think, what you bring to the table, what works best for your group. Yes, there's plenty of support and relevant information in every session. But you choose what to do with it, what works best for your group.

Expect change.

Things are going to happen. The Spirit's at work. You'll never be the same. That's the expectation of this Bible study. Because when you engage God's Word, things change. For you. For your congregation. For the world.

God is on a mission

In No Experience Necessary, you'll open up the Bible and read it for yourself. The most important part of the Bible study is reading from the Bible, listening for God's voice, and talking about what you've read and heard.

As you read the Bible with your small group, you'll see that God has a plan. From the very beginning, God's been on a mission to save and bless the world. We're called to be partners in this mission. God's got work for us to do—work that gives meaning and purpose to our lives.

In each No Experience Necessary Bible study unit, we'll explore the Bible in light of God's mission.

Help Wanted: Unit One

God is on a mission to bless and save the world, and invites us to be partners with God and partners with each other in carrying out this mission. This is the purpose of the Christian life—and our life together as the church.

You're Hired: Unit Two

We're invited to be partners with God and partners with each other in God's mission—a mission that is multifaceted, multidimensional, and utterly holistic, as you'll see in this unit. We're talking about being part of a very BIG project.

SESSION	TITLE	KEY THEME	PRIMARY BIBLE EMPHASIS
1	Re-creation	God invites us to be part of the mission of re-creation.	2 Corinthians 5:11-21
2	Freedom	God invites us to be part of the mission of freedom.	Galatians 5:1-15
3	Justice	God invites us to be part of the mission of justice.	Micah 6:1-8
4	Reconciliation	God invites us to be part of the mission of reconciliation.	Mark 16:1-8
5	Love	God invites us to be part of the mission of love.	John 13:1-35
6	Salvation	God invites us to be part of the mission of salvation.	Luke 2:22-38
7	Disciple-making	God invites us to be part of the mission of disciple-making.	Matthew 4:12-22

On the Job Training: Unit Three

The purpose of the Christian life is to participate in God's mission in the world. This life will be shaped by a set of particular faith practices.

More Than Just a Job: Unit Four

The purpose of our life together is to participate in God's mission in the world. This purpose shapes the way we do everything we do as the church.

Check these out

Be sure to check out other resources in this series:

- *No Experience Necessary: Everybody's Welcome* (Augsburg Fortress, 2005), a revised and expanded edition of the book by Kelly A. Fryer that inspired the Bible study series.
- *No Experience Necessary: Everybody's Welcome Intro VHS/DVD* (Augsburg Fortress, 2005), a video introduction by Kelly A. Fryer, the series author.
- No Experience Necessary Web site (www.noexperiencenecessary.org), a place to find the latest information and order series resources.

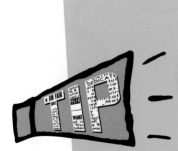

The Bible is available in a variety of sizes, prices, translations, and paraphrases at www.augsburgfortress.org or your local bookstore. No Experience Necessary Bible study primarily uses the New Revised Standard Version (NRSV), but if you have another version of the Bible that you enjoy reading, feel free to use it. Here are two more suggestions: *The Learning Bible: Contemporary English Version* (American Bible Society) and *The Message Remix: The Bible in Contemporary Language* (Navpress, 2003).

Making your group work

You are being invited to answer God's call to follow Jesus into a life that is different...a life that makes a difference in the world.

This is a pretty big deal. And so, although you could do this Bible study by yourself, you might want to consider doing it with a few friends. In a small group, you'll have opportunities to get to know each other, learn from each other, and support each other.

A No Experience Necessary small group can get going with as few as two or three people who want to learn from the Bible and each other. A congregation might start several groups at once or begin a No Experience Necessary Bible study with a group that already exists (for example, a new member class, a women's group, a men's group). However your group comes together, if you have more than a dozen people, consider forming two smaller groups so everyone has a chance to talk.

A team effort

Making a group work takes a team effort. If you are doing this Bible study with others, here's how to help your group to work:

- Think about people you know—family members, friends, neighbors, coworkers—and invite someone to join your group.
- Pray for the group and everyone in it.
- Attend group meetings regularly and bring a Bible if you have one.
- Do your "homework" between sessions, if your group chooses to do this.
- Respect others in the group and make them feel welcome.
- Keep confidential information inside the group.
- Remember that everybody in the group has something to offer.

You'll learn from the Bible and each other.

Facilitators

Every No Experience Necessary group needs a facilitator to encourage discussion and make sure everyone feels welcome. One person might facilitate the group for an entire unit or your group might rotate leadership each week.

The facilitator isn't expected to be an expert. In fact, it's the facilitator's job to NOT be the expert in the discussion. Everybody has something to offer, but people won't offer it if they're looking to one person for all the "right" answers.

If you are a facilitator in No Experience Necessary, here are additional ways that you help your group to work:

- Tell others about your group and invite them to join. Be sure to let them know when and where you are meeting.
- Make group meetings a high priority.
- Distribute the No Experience Necessary Bible study and *No Experience Necessary: Everybody's Welcome* book to the group.
- Read each session, including the main Bible passage and "Group Tips," ahead of time. "Group Tips" gives you suggestions for leading your group through the material.
- Make sure your group has a relaxed and inviting place to meet with good lighting, plenty of seating, and light refreshments if you choose. Arrange chairs in a circle, if at all possible, so group members can see and hear each other. Ask everyone to turn off cell phone ringers during the sessions.
- Allow time for questions.
- Give everyone a chance to talk without making anyone feel like she or he has to talk or allowing one person to do all the talking.
- Don't do it all. Give members of your group opportunities to set up chairs, talk, pray out loud, read, choose what to do next, make coffee, bring cookies, and so on. Everyone has something to offer.
- Encourage the group to have fun!
- Remind the group why it's there—to open up the Bible and read it together, discover what God is doing in the passage, and listen for what God has to say. That's the main focus for every session.

More resources for facilitators

- Read all of "Everybody's Welcome" (pages 4-7) and "Making Your Group Work" (pages 8-15) as an introduction to the Bible study and your role.
- Read the book *No Experience Necessary: Everybody's Welcome* (Augsburg Fortress, 2005) for more background on what the Bible is about and the ideas behind the Bible study.
- Visit the No Experience Necessary Web site at www.noexperience necessary.org for the latest information on the series.
- Remember that everyone has something to offer. You'll learn from the Bible and each other.
- Rely on the Holy Spirit to guide and challenge you and your group as you listen for God's voice together.

How to get the most out of each session

The "Group Tips" throughout each session provide suggestions for using the following session components with your group.

Come as you are

This is a time to get to know one another, make everybody feel welcome, and begin to build trust within the group.

Start each session by checking in with each other. Invite everyone to briefly share how things are going or get conversation started with the suggestions provided in "Group Tips."

After checking in, read the opening paragraph(s) in the "Come As You Are" section, then take time to pray together. Do this on your own or use the prayer provided in the session.

Just 3 questions

Everything in the session builds on the Bible passage and the three questions located here, so be sure to spend the most time on this section every time you meet.

Read the Bible passage out loud and discuss the following questions about the reading.

1|What do you think God is doing here? (In other words, what's going on in this reading? What's God up to? What's the plot of the story? Who are the characters and what are they up to?)

2|What do you hear God saying to you, personally? (What is God saying to you about your life, relationships, work, and so on in this reading? What is God saying to you about what you're called to be or to do?)

3|What do you hear God saying to us (as a small group, congregation, community, nation)? (How is God calling, challenging, directing, forgiving, and loving us in this reading? What is God saying about what we're called to be or to do?)

God is speaking to each one of us, so everyone has something to offer in this discussion. You'll learn from the Bible and each other.

Heart of the matter

This section contains the "lead article" in each session. The lead article draws out themes and gives you additional ways to talk about the main Bible passage.

In "Heart of the Matter," you'll read the lead article and discuss it, using the question(s) found at the end of the article.

Another look; Right to the point; Bible basics; and Right here, Right now

These four sections include "feature articles" that look at the main Bible passage from different angles. Pick one or two of these articles to read, either out loud or to yourself. Then discuss them, using the questions at the end of the articles.

Don't expect your group to get through all of the feature articles included in a session. There are more than enough articles here for your time together, so choose the ones your group is most interested in. (Everyone can read the rest of the articles on their own during the week.)

Get going

No matter how many feature articles you use in the session, close with "Get Going."

Here you'll read the "Wrap Up" article and discuss the question at the end. Then plan for your next meeting. End the session by praying together on your own or use the suggestions provided in this section.

Invite people to join No Experience Necessary.

Exercise your options

You have multiple options in No Experience Necessary, so feel free to use the Bible study in any way that makes sense for your group.

The time and place for your meetings

Most groups find it helpful to have a regular time and place to meet. Meet Sunday mornings at church, Thursday nights with coffee and cookies in someone's home, Saturdays over breakfast in a restaurant, or at another time and place that works for your group.

The length of your sessions

Make sure everyone in the group knows in advance how long the meetings will run. You can meet for 60 minutes, 90 minutes, or for a longer time if the group chooses. Here are suggestions for using your time together.

	60 MINUTES	90 MINUTES	120 MINUTES
Come as you are	10 minutes	15 minutes	15 minutes
Just 3 questions	20 minutes	30 minutes	40 minutes
Heart of the matter	10 minutes	10 minutes	15 minutes
Another look; Right to the point; Bible basics; Right here, right now	15 minutes	30 minutes	40 minutes
Get going	5 minutes	5 minutes	10 minutes

The material covered in your sessions

Focus on reading the main Bible passage and discussing the three questions. Then read the lead article and talk about it. If you have time, read and discuss as many feature articles as you want.

Every person involved in the Bible study should have *No Experience Necessary: Everybody's Welcome* (Augsburg Fortress, 2005). Decide how you'll use the book as a group. You can decide to read a couple of chapters during the course of each Bible study unit or, if you wish, read the entire book at once and refer back to it during each unit. Discuss the book in your regular meetings or schedule an extra meeting or two to talk only about the book.

"Homework" done between sessions

As everybody in the group gets more and more involved in discussion, you'll probably find that each session contains more feature articles than you can cover in one meeting. That's great! Read the rest of the articles on your own during the week. If you want, you can talk about what you've read as you check in at the next meeting. Or decide as a group to read the main Bible passage or one of the articles for the next session in advance. Of course, your group also has the option to not do any homework between sessions.

The *No Experience Necessary: Everybody's Welcome Intro* VHS or DVD (Augsburg Fortress, 2005)

Schedule a special "kickoff" meeting for your group to view the VHS or DVD and learn about the series. If your congregation is starting more than one No Experience Necessary group, you might hold a combined "kickoff" for members of all the groups. Also, consider using the video to invite people to join No Experience Necessary:

- Show all or part of the video before or after worship or at other gatherings in your congregation.
- Loan the video to friends and neighbors and invite them to join your group.
- Invite members of your congregation and community to a "No Experience Necessary Night" and encourage people to bring their friends, family members, neighbors, and coworkers. Set up tables and place a sign-up form for No Experience Necessary groups on each one. After a light supper or snack, show the video and then spend some time in discussion.

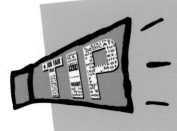

Whether or not you have read and studied the Bible before, watch for "Tips" like this one. They will help you read and interpret Bible passages on your own.

A Letter from Kelly

Bible study is way more fun—and meaningful—if you're not trying to do it alone. That's why *this* Bible study is encouraging you to join—or start!—a No Experience Necessary small group of your own.

But this isn't just a practical tip for how to get the most out of your Bible reading. This is a theological issue. You see, God's Word comes to us in several different ways. That's because God's Word is alive! Jesus Christ is *the Word made flesh* (John 1). And Jesus, through the Holy Spirit, is still very much at work right here. Right now. The Word of God could never be contained in a single book or captured on a written page. It is more dynamic than that. God is still speaking! We hear God speak to us in the words of a Sunday morning sermon and in the clear, confident declaration of forgiveness. God speaks to us in a way that goes *beyond all words* in a bit of broken bread, shared together at the Lord's table, and in a baptismal splash. God speaks to us through the voice of a caring and wise friend who, in the midst of our darkness, promises that light will shine again one day. I have heard God speak to me through my children, in their innocent and true pronouncement: "I love you, Mom. And God loves you too."

In the Bible, God speaks to us in a very special way. That's why the Bible is the norm for our life together as Christians. That's why we turn to the Bible for guidance in all things.

> God's Word comes to us in several different ways. That's because God's Word is alive!

But the Bible is not the only way God speaks to us. And we miss out on something really important when we aren't listening for what God has to say to us...*through each other.*

My partner in writing this second unit of the No Experience Necessary Bible study is Rolf Jacobson. Rolf teaches Old Testament at Luther Seminary in St. Paul, Minnesota. As a consultant on Unit One, he taught me a lot about the most current thinking in biblical scholarship. He was also one of the key people in the background, telling me when I was being too confusing or too long-winded or just plain wrong about something. Rolf particularly seemed to enjoy this job. That's partly why I invited him to join me in actually writing Unit Two. Rolf knows his stuff. But he also knows how to say things in a way that make sense even to somebody like me. And he has a wicked sense of humor! Rolf wrote about half the articles in this unit and a couple of the "Right Here, Right Now" stories. Having a partner in writing this Bible study has been great. I think I'd be missing out on something really important if I was trying to do it alone.

That's how it works when it comes to the Bible. It's meant to be read and studied and reflected upon *in partnership* with other people.

If you don't have a No Experience Necessary small group yet, start one yourself. Don't wait for somebody to put a program together for you. Grab a friend or two. Set a date and time. Find a place (preferably somewhere with food). And go to work. Don't worry about "doing it right" or knowing all the answers. God will show up.

That's a promise.

We miss out on something really important when we aren't listening for what God has to say to us... *through each other.*

1 RE-CREATION

God invites us to be part of
the mission of re-creation.

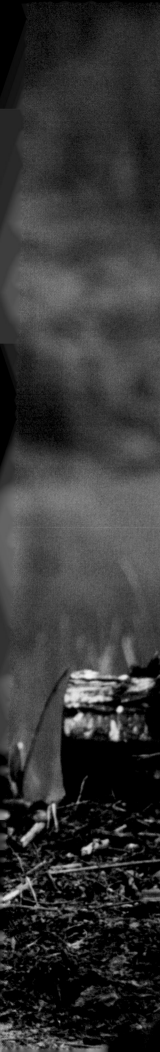

COME AS YOU ARE

In the beginning, God created the world and everything in it. From that moment, humans have been doing everything possible to wreck it. But God loves this world. And God loves us. That's why God's mission is to put this wonderful—but broken—world back together again. What's more, God invites you and me to be a part of this re-creation mission. That's what the apostle Paul told the Christians who belonged to the early church in Corinth.

Spend some time getting to know one another before you dive into the study. Introduce yourselves. Talk about why you're at this No Experience Bible study and what you hope to get out of it. Then pray together. In the next session, we'll start inviting group members to offer "free-form" prayers, but for this first session, just pray this prayer out loud together:

Gracious God, thank you for gathering us together. Help us to be open to the new things we might learn from your Word and from each other. Re-create us and make us new! In Jesus' name. Amen

JUST 3 QUESTIONS

Open your Bibles to 2 Corinthians 5:11-21. Take turns reading this passage, a verse or two at a time, out loud. Then spend some time talking about what is happening in this passage, including what you are hearing God say here. Use these three questions as a starting point to have this conversation:

1 | **What do you think God is doing here?**

2 | **What do you hear God saying to you, personally?**

3 | **What do you hear God saying to us (as a small group, congregation, community, nation)?**

"Group Tips" is here to help a facilitator guide this Bible study with a small group. See pages 4-17 for more on this. Your group can choose one facilitator or rotate leadership with each session.

COME AS YOU ARE

Spend time getting to know each other. You might try this discussion starter: "What have you 'created' that you are really proud of?"

Spend a little time discussing how you want your group to work. You could even list some "ground rules." For example:
1) There are no experts! We all have something to offer.
2) Respect one another's opinions!
3) Everything that gets said in the group STAYS in the group!

Talk about what you hope to get out of the group too. Make sure everyone has a chance to share her or his thoughts on this.

JUST 3 QUESTIONS

Absolutely the most important part of your time together will be the time you spend reading and talking about the Bible. God has something to say to you in these words! Be open to hearing God's voice through the words you read…and through each other. The idea that we can hear God speaking might seem weird at first, so be patient with each other and with yourself. You'll get the hang of it.

All things new

HEART OF THE MATTER

Give each other time to quietly read the "Heart of the Matter" article titled "All Things New" (unless you all agreed to read it during the past week). Then take a few minutes to talk about it. Use the discussion question at the end of the article to get you going.

L et's face it: there are few things people are better at than wrecking stuff. And this isn't new. It's not like it used to be better back in the "good old days." There never were any "good old days." As far back as we can go, we find evidence that wrecking stuff is part of human nature. Remember Adam and Eve? They managed to wreck paradise!

The good news is that, even though we seem incapable of not wrecking everything—from our most important relationships to the beauty of creation— God is even more determined to put things back together again. And we are invited to be a part of that mission.

A hoped-for tomorrow

One way the Bible describes God's mission is *re-creation*. In other words, God is *making new* the important things we humans have gotten all messed up.

This was especially good news for Paul, who wrote this letter to the Christians in the city of Corinth. Paul had lived in Corinth and, while working there as a tent maker, had planted this church. He loved these people. They loved him too. And even after he left, he kept up a close relationship with them through letter writing. But at some point, news reached Paul that the church was in trouble. They had been visited by some Christian missionaries who had very different views. These missionaries criticized Paul and turned some people in the church against him. Paul dropped what he was doing and went back to Corinth. This second visit, Paul himself said, was "painful" (2 Corinthians 2:1). It was followed by a letter of "many tears" (2:4). His relationship with the church at Corinth, once so important to Paul, was the very definition of *wrecked*. In fact, Paul was so upset that he knew he appeared beside himself (5:13).

But Paul knew something important. He knew nothing in all creation is so broken that God can't fix it. Paul believed with all his heart that one day

> God is *making new* the important things we humans have gotten all messed up.

> Jesus makes it possible for us to live right now as if that promised future is already here.

everything would be made right again, not only this broken relationship with his friends, but everything! This gave him the confidence to keep going, no matter how much suffering or disappointment or hardship he encountered.

A brand new today

But Paul also knew that God's promise of "one day" was not just a future reality. It could be, even if for brief moments at a time, experienced right here. Right now. "If anyone is in Christ," Paul exclaimed, "there is a new creation: everything old has passed away; see, everything has become new!" (5:17).

In other words, Jesus makes it possible for us to live right now as if that promised future is already here. In Christ, enemies can become friends. Broken trust can be restored. Old wounds can be healed. Empty stomachs can be filled. Those imprisoned—by fear or hatred or self-loathing or greed or lust or anything else—can be set free. Out of the wreckage we cause at every

turn, something new can emerge. We can be more than home-wreckers, heartbreakers, planet-destroyers. We can be who God says we already are, through Jesus Christ! We can live the new life God says we have already been given!

A message to share

Knowing that God was making all things new gave Paul strength and confidence. And he wanted everyone to know this. I am an "ambassador" (5:20) of this good news, he said. It was his job to tell all people that they are not stuck in the wreckage of their lives.

That's not a bad way to describe the job you and I have been given, either.

As you look around at the world— or at your life—what do you hope will one day be "made new"? What can you do to help make that happen? What can your group or congregation do?

An old, old message

First, God created the universe and everything that exists. Then sin entered into the world and messed up God's creation. Ever since then God has been working to re-create the good creation, to fashion it back into the way it was meant to be. When Jesus showed up, God extended the work of new creation to all the earth and all people.

Keep in mind that God was re-creating long before Jesus. In the Old Testament (the books of the Bible that tell of God's dealings with Israel before the time of Jesus) there are many examples of this. *Read an example of God's re-creating work in Ezekiel 37:1-14 right now.*

Ezekiel's message was a message of hope.

Ezekiel was one of God's prophets. A prophet was not someone who predicted the future. A prophet was a person, sent by God, who delivered messages from God to God's people about the here and now.

Ezekiel lived at a tumultuous time in Israel's history. He was born in Jerusalem just before that city rebelled against King Nebuchadnezzar (pronounced *Neh-bah-cah-NEZ-ur*) of Babylon. Nebuchadnezzar was the power every other nation had to deal with. Unfortunately, he was also an angry guy. He was not amused by Jerusalem's little rebellion. Nebuchadnezzar destroyed the city and forced many of its leaders to walk all the way to Babylon where they were forced to live. Ezekiel was one of those who was forced into exile.

Stuck in Babylon, Ezekiel's people had given up all hope. Ezekiel quotes them as saying, "Our bones are dried up, and our hope is gone, we are cut off from God!" And that's when God sent Ezekiel a vision of a valley full of dead, dry bones. Then God sent a *ruach* (*ROO-awk*, which in Hebrew can mean "breath," "wind," or "spirit") into the bones and those bones lived, breathed, and walked around.

Ezekiel's message was a message of hope. God was announcing to the people that no matter how bad things looked, as long as the Holy Spirit was in them as a people they could live. Indeed, God was promising that God would do a new thing in them. God would re-create them!

How do you think people would respond to Ezekiel if he showed up and told people about his "vision" today?

GROUP TIPS

After you've finished talking about the "Heart of the Matter" article, browse through the rest of the session. Pick one or two additional articles from "Another Look," "Right to the Point," "Bible Basics," or "Right Here, Right Now." Read these articles out loud or silently. Then talk about them. Use the discussion questions to spark your conversation.

You most likely will not get through all of the articles, so pick the ones your group is most interested in. Encourage group members to read the rest of the articles on their own during the week.

ANOTHER LOOK

"Another Look" explores this session's theme from the perspective of another book in the Bible.

Have everyone who is willing take turns reading Ezekiel 37:1-14.

An open curtain

Remember that climactic scene in *The Wizard of Oz* when Dorothy and company arrive back at the Emerald City with news of their success—much to the wizard's dismay—and the dog Toto unveils the wizard's secret identity?

> I am nothing but a "clay jar," Paul says. Easily chipped and broken. Not much to look at. Not worth much at all. I am who I am only because God's extraordinary power is at work in me.

"Pay no attention to the man behind the curtain!" the wizard shouts in desperation. But it's too late. He is revealed, once and for all, as a shady fortune-teller from Kansas.

You might expect somebody with the reputation of "St. Paul" to feel just as embarrassed about having the whole world see through his public image. But Paul doesn't wait for Toto to come along. He pulls the curtain aside himself.

Read 2 Corinthians 4:7-15 right now and see for yourself.

I am nothing but a "clay jar," Paul says. Easily chipped and broken. Not much to look at. Not worth much at all. I am who I am only because God's extraordinary power is at work in me. Every time I get beaten down, God lifts me up. Every time I am confused, God sets me straight. Every time I think I am at the end of my rope, God helps me hang on. And, when this life is over, I know I will live with Jesus forever. Whatever "treasure" you might see within me, Paul says, is all God's doing. God does this "so that the life of Jesus may also be made visible" in me (4:10). In other words, when people see the new "me," *they are really seeing the God who made me new!*

Paul was God's *messenger*, carrying the good news of God's power to make all things new. Even more, through Paul, people could *see* God's power at work. "In Christ, there is a new creation" (5:17)! That was true about Paul. It is true about you and me and the community of faith—the church—to which we belong.

Through us, people should be able to see the amazing God who makes all things new. As we give generously, help people who are poor, and live in harmony and peace, the world will see the power of God.

Tell about a person through whom you have seen God's power at work. Have you ever felt God's power at work through you? If so, how did you feel about this?

Paul actually wrote at least four letters to the church in Corinth. Here is a guess at how these letters unfolded:

1 | Paul's first writing (this letter didn't survive)
2 | The Corinthians responded
3 | Paul's second writing (this is now 1 Corinthians)
4 | The Corinthians responded
5 | Paul's third writing (this letter didn't survive)
6 | The Corinthians responded
7 | Paul's fourth writing (this is now 2 Corinthians)

What is re-creation?

Perhaps the two most important skills for interpreting the Bible are 1) learning to ask good questions and 2) learning how to follow up on those questions. An example of a basic question is: "What does re-creation mean?" Obviously, to be re-created is a *metaphor*

for what God does to us through Christ. That is, in re-creation God does not *literally* rebuild our DNA, RNA, and cellular structure. So, then, what is re-creation?

That's how you ask a good question.

And if you want to learn to answer a question like that, here is what you should NOT do: *Rely only on an expert*. It is okay to ask your pastor or favorite Bible "expert," but be confident n your own abilities too!

One good way to answer your own questions is to use the notes in a study Bible. Caution: I said *use* the notes. I did not say believe everything in the notes. The notes, after all, are just what one Bible scholar wrote. But often there is good information in those notes for you to think about (emphasis on *you* and emphasis on *think about*!). God gave you a brain and trusts you to use it—especially when you are reading God's Word.

If, for example, you went to a study Bible with the question, "What does re-creation mean?" it would probably point you to other places in the Bible where re-creation is discussed. My study Bible suggests passages in Isaiah, Galatians, Romans, Ephesians, 2 Peter,

> **God gave you a brain and trusts you to use it— especially when you are reading God's Word.**

and Revelation. You could read them all. Or you could just read the passages in Galatians and Romans. Why? Because those are letters which were also written by Paul, the same person who wrote 2 Corinthians. (Note: Passages in which *the same author* discusses similar ideas are a little more closely connected than passages that discuss *the same ideas* but were written by different authors.)

So go ahead and *read Galatians 6:15 and Romans 8:19-23* right now. Read a little before and a little after in order to get some context on those passages. Think about them! If you get excited, read the notes about them in a study Bible.

Oh...don't wait for me (your friendly neighborhood Bible nerd) to tell you what it means to be "re-created"! God loves it when you use your own brain... especially for thinking about God's Word.

Does the idea that God wants you to "think for yourself" about the Bible excite you? Intimidate you? Or something else?

RIGHT TO THE POINT

"Right to the Point" goes deeper into this session's theme or explores it from a different angle.

Take turns reading 2 Corinthians 4:7-15.

BIBLE BASICS

"Bible Basics" will help you learn more about how to read and understand the Bible.

Take turns reading Galations 6:15 and Romans 8:19-23.

Rolf A. Jacobson

The old guard

On October 26, 1980, I confirmed my Christian faith at St. John's Lutheran Church in Northfield, Minnesota. Among those present that morning were many friends, classmates, and relatives—to whom I paid significant attention, because I knew them personally.

Also present were many older members of the congregation—to whom I paid little attention, because I didn't really know them.

Three Sundays later, I was tossing the football in the front yard with my father, when my father asked our next-door neighbor—who was also our family doctor—to take a look at a problem I was having with my right leg.

The next day, I went to the Mayo Clinic for consultation. The day after that, I was admitted to the hospital at Mayo. The day after that, the surgeons amputated my right leg. The problem that I was having was diagnosed as cancer and amputation was the solution.

The day after that, cards and letters started arriving. Many cards came from friends, classmates, and relatives. But even more cards came from older members of my congregation. People who didn't know me personally—but who knew my family. And more importantly, they knew God.

Over the next three years, my other leg was also amputated, I had nine lung surgeries, and underwent both chemotherapy and radiation. And all the while, I kept receiving cards, letters, calls, and prayers from those older members of the congregation who knew Jesus.

What were those older folks doing? They were responding to God's love and joining God's mission of *re-creation*. In many ways, my old life was over—dead. My legs were gone; there would be no more running, jumping, dancing, playing sports, marching in the band, or even standing at the altar to receive communion.

But God was there in my life, creating a new future. And those older members were there, praying, serving, encouraging, and believing me into that new creation.

Who does God want to send you to with a message of encouragement and new life?

Those older members were there, praying, serving, encouraging, and believing me into that new creation.

"Creator" is not just a job description for God, it is part of God's very identity. We believe in God the Father almighty, creator of heaven and earth. And the act of creation is not just a onetime event that was over and done with. God continues to create right now. And at the end of time, God will create a new universe too.

Wrap up

From the beginning, God has been creating and re-creating! That is who God IS. That is what God DOES. But that's not the only way to describe the mission God is on. For next week, read Galatians 5:1-15, and explore another way to describe God's mission.

What key ideas are you taking home from this session?

Before you go, pray the Lord's Prayer together out loud:

Our Father in heaven,
Hallowed be your name,
Your kingdom come,
Your will be done,
On earth as in heaven.
Give us today our daily bread.
Forgive us our sins
As we forgive those who sin against us.
Save us from the time of trial
And deliver us from evil.
For the kingdom, the power,
And the glory are yours,
Now and forever. Amen

GROUP TIPS

RIGHT HERE, RIGHT NOW

"Right Here, Right Now" connects this session's theme with real life.

GET GOING

Read "Wrap Up" out loud or silently. Then take turns answering the question.

Decide as a group if you will do any "homework" for the coming week. Before the next meeting, group members could read all of Session 2 or at least the lead article ("Heart of the Matter") and the main Bible passage.

As a group, also consider reading at least chapters 3-4 in the book *No Experience Necessary: Everybody's Welcome* (Augsburg Fortress, 2005) as you go through this unit.

End by praying together. This might be uncomfortable for some people in your group. Don't ever make people do anything they are not comfortable doing! Make sure everyone has space to participate at her or his own pace. In fact, since this is the first session of "You're Hired," you might want to end by simply praying the Lord's Prayer together.

2|FREEDOM

God invites us to be part of
the mission of freedom.

COME AS YOU ARE

The more you get to know Paul—famous apostle, church planter, letter writer—the more you'll discover a guy who always speaks his mind. When he is excited about something—or upset—you know it. Paul had started the churches in a region called Galatia. He loved the Christians there. But early on in a letter to them, he yells, "You foolish Galatians!" (Galatians 3:1). He was hopping mad. These Christians had allowed themselves to be made servants of something other than Christ. They had become slaves to "the law," of all things. Paul sets them straight. And, frankly, we could use a little of Paul's straight talking, truth telling today. God is on a mission to set us free from *anything* that would enslave and kill us if we'd let it.

Before you go too much further, spend some time checking in with each other. If yours is a new group, get to know each other better. Do this however you want or use this discussion starter: "Who has been a straight talker and truth teller in your life? Have you been thankful for this person? Why or why not?"

After you've checked in, pray together. If someone is willing to offer a "free-form" prayer, asking the Holy Spirit to be present during your study time, great! At the end of that prayer, everyone could pray this prayer out loud together:

Dear God, thank you for bringing us together to study and learn. Help us hear your voice. Teach us something new. Bless our time together. In Jesus' name. Amen

JUST 3 QUESTIONS

Open your Bibles to Galatians 5:1-15. Take turns reading this passage, a verse or two at a time, out loud. Then spend some time talking about what is happening in this passage, including what you are hearing God say here. Use these three questions as a starting point to have this conversation:

1 | What do you think God is doing here?

2 | What do you hear God saying to you, personally?

3 | What do you hear God saying to us (as a small group, congregation, community, nation)?

GROUP TIPS

Remember, if you are facilitating this group, see pages 4-17 for further suggestions on using this material.

COME AS YOU ARE

This time sets the tone for the rest of the session. There are a lot of ways groups "check in" with each other, so choose what makes sense for your group. Be sure to listen to each other. Invite the quietest members to participate. Remind each other that whatever gets said in the group STAYS in the group. Smile a lot and laugh together. Have fun!

Ask for a volunteer who would feel comfortable praying out loud briefly in her or his own words. Each session will include time for "free-form" prayer like this. Encourage everyone to offer a prayer at some time in this unit, but don't force anyone to do so.

JUST 3 QUESTIONS

Absolutely the most important part of your time together will be the time you spend reading and talking about the Bible. God has something to say to you in these words! Be open to hearing God's voice through the words you read…and through each other. Be patient with each other and with yourself. Listen for what God is saying.

Free at last!

When you've finished talking about the three questions, give each other time to quietly read the "Heart of the Matter" article titled "Free at Last!" (unless you all agreed to read it during the past week). Then take a few minutes to talk about it. Use the discussion questions at the end of the article to get you going.

We get *enslaved* to all sorts of weird things. *Enslaved* isn't a word we're used to in everyday conversation, of course. But that's the best word to describe what it's like for somebody who is trying to quit smoking, for example. Have you been there? Then you know it's true. It's true about all kinds of things: fast food, fast cars, a quick buck. We get enslaved to our possessions (and squeezed to death by credit card debt), to our homes (i.e., "money pits"), and to our jobs. Some of us even talk about feeling "chained to our desks." We get enslaved to everything from crack cocaine to mind-numbing television. Weird, maybe. And dumb. But true.

Underneath all of this odd and self-destructive behavior is a desire to be bigger and better and safer and more powerful. We want to be in control. It's a terrible thing, then, when we wake up to discover that these things have quietly and completely taken control of us.

A strange addiction

Back around the time of Jesus, one of the things people (religious people, anyway) allowed themselves to be enslaved to was "the law." This was especially tricky to get out of because the law had been given by God.

> **They [the laws] weren't meant to be unchanging and they weren't supposed to be a burden.**

Through Moses, God had given the 10 Commandments and other laws designed to bring order into people's lives. These laws were dynamic, changing over time to address the needs of real people living in very different contexts. (That's why we no longer teach "You shall not muzzle an ox while it is treading out the grain" [Deuteronomy 25:4]. Whatever *that* means!) Changes in the law take place within the Bible itself. God wanted laws to make sense in each new generation. They weren't meant to be unchanging and they weren't supposed to be a burden. These laws are a sign that God is near enough to care about even the smallest details of our life together (Deuteronomy 4:5-8)!

Somehow, though, many people in Jesus' time (like people in every time and place) managed to turn the gift of the law into a burden. In other words, they

> If you're going to give yourself away to anything, serve Christ by giving yourself away to your neighbors.

believed you would be acceptable to God *if* you did what you were supposed to do (big emphasis on *if*).

Well, Paul knew there are no "ifs, ands, or buts" about it. God sent Jesus to save sinners! God doesn't give the law so we can *earn* God's acceptance. God gives us laws to order our lives because God loves us.

But addiction to the law was a hard habit to break.

Freedom from it all!

It was hard, even for those people who became Christians, to shake this idea that *keeping the law* is the most important thing. Paul did his best to teach people this wasn't how it worked. But then the Christians in Galatia started requiring adult men (who hadn't been raised according to "the law") to be circumcised in order to join the church. And Paul's blood pressure went through the roof.

I wish those who are telling you these things, Paul yelled, would just "castrate themselves" (Galatians 5:12). You don't have to keep the law to be acceptable to God! You are made acceptable to God through Jesus Christ. Have faith in Christ! And him alone.

Christ sets us free from every bondage, every addiction, every false god. Because of Jesus, we are even set free from death! Clinging to anything except Christ is just foolishness. Nothing else— not our jobs, our homes, our possessions, not even "the law"— can save us.

Freedom for service

As wonderful as this good news is, though, we would continue to give ourselves away to all kinds of weird things. That's just how we are. And so Paul invites us to do this: If you're going to give yourself away to anything, serve Christ by giving yourself away to your neighbors. Do whatever you can to share this good news with them. Be an encourager. Be a helper. Be a friend. Let the people in your life meet Jesus through you. You have been set free.

Let them know this gift is for them too.

Do you think it's true that people get "enslaved" to all sorts of things today? What does that look like? What does it look like in your life? Why do we do this?

True freedom

What does it mean to be *freed*? What does it mean to live as a *free person*? Most of us think we know the answer to these questions. If we were asked "What does freedom mean?" we'd say, "Freedom means we get to do what we want to do."

But we have something to learn from the Bible. In the Bible, freedom means that because of the grace of God, we get to live the way *God* wants us to live!

> **In the Bible, freedom means that because of the grace of God, we get to live the way *God* wants us to live!**

The story of freedom par excellence in the Bible is the story of the exodus—when God brought the children of Israel out of the land of Egypt, where they had been slaves. God *freed* them. But they had been slaves for so long—hundreds of years, according to the Bible—that they had no idea how to live as *free people*.

So God said this: "You don't know how to live as a free person? That's okay, I am with you and I will help you. I'll make you a list. This is how free people live." And then God gave them a list:

- I will be your God and you will be my people. To be free is to know me.
- Do not worship anything else.
- Use my name to pray and praise, but do not misuse my name.
- Take one day off of work each week—use it for worship and for family, and make sure you give those who are poor a day off too.
- Honor your mother and father, especially when they get old.
- Do not murder.
- Do not have sex with anyone other than your spouse.
- Do not steal.
- Do not use your words to hurt your neighbor, even if you think you are telling the truth about your neighbor.
- Do not desire your neighbor's stuff.

And that, according to God, is how free people live. We don't just run around doing whatever we want to do. Rather, we do what *God* wants us to do. And when we do that, we know what true freedom is.

Has there ever been a time in your life when you just ran around doing whatever you wanted to do? How'd that work out for you?

"Freedom" is not just about being freed from sin. In the Bible, God's freedom also has to do with political and worldly matters. God freed the people of Israel from slavery to Pharaoh. God remains deeply concerned and involved with the struggles of all people to be free—especially to be free to worship the living Lord who raised Jesus from the dead.

GROUP TIPS

After you've finished talking about the "Heart of the Matter" article, browse through the rest of the session. Pick one or two additional articles from "Another Look," "Right to the Point," "Bible Basics," or "Right Here, Right Now." Read these articles out loud or silently. Then talk about them. Use the discussion questions to spark your conversation.

You most likely will not get through all of the articles, so pick the ones your group is most interested in. Encourage group members to read the rest of the articles on their own during the week.

ANOTHER LOOK

"Another Look" explores this session's theme from the perspective of another book in the Bible.

We've never done it that way before!

Paul wasn't kidding when he said that Christ sets us free. *Read Galatians 3:23-28* right now for a glimpse into the radical nature of the freedom Paul is talking about.

In Paul's day, there were pretty clear lines dividing people from each other. If you were a Jew, for example, you tried not to mix with Gentiles (people who weren't Jews). It was a problem to eat with them or visit in their homes. People

lived within a pretty strict hierarchical system too. Men had all the power; women didn't have any. And slaves were...well, they were slaves. Nobody ever really questioned these things. It was just the way it had always been done.

But in Christ, Paul said, not even "the way we've always done it" can hold us captive.

Christ came to us humbly and in the form of a servant. This is the one who breaks down the barriers we build up between "us" and "them." Christ erases all of our dividing lines. He dismantles oppressive hierarchies. He makes it clear that even the lowliest and poorest person has immense value in God's eyes. He sets us free to create whole new relationships with one another within the Christian community.

Because of Jesus, our old ways of relating to one another just won't cut it anymore. That's especially true in the church. But it is also true, for those of us who are Christians, in our homes and in our workplaces and in our communities.

There can be no more lines dividing us from one another. We are free to love and serve each other, just as Jesus came to love and serve. We are all children of God.

Every single one of us.

Every single one.

> **Christ erases all of our dividing lines.**

> What would it look like if we really believed we were free to do—and be—a new thing in our homes, workplaces, and congregation?

Piecing it together

Have you ever listened to one side of a phone conversation? If you have, you know that in order not to jump to false conclusions, you have to piece together the other side of the conversation. When we read Paul's letters, that's exactly what we have to do. We are reading public (not private!) letters that Paul wrote to real people, who had real questions about real issues. But we're only getting one side of the story.

A key thing to understanding Paul's letters is to try to piece together the issues and questions he was writing about. For the original readers, the Christian life was like an unmapped, unexplored world. They knew what Jesus had done for them—given his life to set them free. But they did not always know what that freedom was all about. What were they free to do— and not to do?

> **A key thing to understanding Paul's letters is to try to piece together the issues and questions he was writing about.**

Based on clues in Paul's letter to the Galatians, one of the issues was whether Christians still needed to keep God's law, as given in the Old Testament. Paul taught that, in Christ, we find freedom from the law. But some other Christians were telling the Galatians that in order to be a Christian, a person still needed to keep the law. Paul said these "false believers" (Galatians 2:4) were preaching "a different gospel" (1:6), likely teaching that Christian males had to be "circumcised" (2:3-5; 5:2-12) and needed to obey "special [holy] days, and months, and season, and years" (4:10).

Paul's big question is this: If Christ died for us, then why would we have to do any of these things? Was Christ's death not enough? Do we need to improve upon Christ's death by adding something to it, such as circumcision or obedience to holy days? Paul shouted: No! Whether we do or do not keep the law can't change what Jesus did for us. Paul even wrote: "If justification [being reconciled to God] comes through the law, then Christ died for nothing" (2:21).

So that tells us what we are free *not to do*. But what are we free *to do*? Paul says we are free to love our neighbor, especially our neighbor who is poor. Paul wrote that Peter and John and the other disciples "asked only one thing, that we remember the poor" (2:10). And Paul wrote "Use your freedom as an opportunity" not for self-indulgence, but rather to show love to the neighbor (5:13).

Paul's letters were written a long time ago to particular people about particular issues. What (if any) difference does that make in how we should read them today?

GROUP TIPS

RIGHT TO THE POINT

"Right to the Point" goes deeper into this session's theme or explores it from a different angle.

Have everyone who is willing take turns reading Galatians 3:23-28.

BIBLE BASICS

"Bible Basics" will help you learn more about how to read and understand the Bible.

Kelly A. Fryer

Rick

Thanks for meeting me," Rick said. He had asked me to meet him for lunch at a bar near his office. The bartender said hello to him by name when we walked in. Rick introduced me as his pastor.

"I'm thinking about selling the business," he said. "I'm just sick and tired of it."

In fact, Rick was miserable. He was sick and tired of everything. His business had never been in better shape. His wife was devoted to him. His oldest son had gone off to college on an athletic scholarship and was getting great grades. His youngest son, in his first year of high school, was handsome, smart, and popular. Rick had built an incredible home. He and his family vacationed multiple times a year, at the most enviable locations. There was nothing this guy didn't have. And he was ready to chuck it all in.

We had been having this conversation, or conversations similar to it, for as long as I had known him. And I gave him the same response every time: "Rick, it's time for you to get serious about tithing."

Rick and his family were among the biggest supporters of the congregation. They were giving away a lot of money every year, but nowhere near 10 percent of their income. And, obviously, it wasn't having much impact on their lifestyle.

"In fact, I'm not sure 10 percent is even enough," I said. "You need to give away as much as it takes for you to really *feel* it."

> **All the stuff Rick has actually belongs to *God*. And God wants to use Rick's stuff to get some really important things done in the world.**

I didn't say it this way, exactly, but the truth is that Rick wasn't doing much more than "tipping" God. It was a nice way of saying thanks to God for the great service. But Rick still believed that everything he had really belonged to *him* and he, therefore, had a right to do with it whatever he wanted. No wonder he was bored.

All the stuff Rick has actually belongs to *God*. And God wants to use Rick's stuff to get some really important things done in the world. God wants to be at work *through* Rick, making a mark and making a difference. Now, *that* would be a life worth living.

Rick looked as unconvinced as ever. He paid the bill and left a generous tip.

"See you Sunday," he said, as he drove away with the top down on his newest toy.

Maybe it was my imagination, but I thought Rick looked just a little more sad than usual.

Why is it so much easier to become slaves to our "stuff" than to use our "stuff" to serve God? Would we be happier if we got it right? Why or why not?

Wrap up

G od is on a mission to set people free from anything and everything that threatens to enslave and kill us. But this is NOT freedom to do whatever we want. It is freedom to do what God wants. For next week, read Micah 6:1-8 and come prepared to learn more about what it is, exactly, that God wants.

We are set free to serve Christ by serving our neighbors. How will you do this in the next week?

Before you go, pray together out loud. Have somebody offer a free-form prayer. Then pray this prayer together:

Loving God, thank you for setting us free to serve you. Be with us during our week. Use our stuff—and our lives— to make a difference. In Jesus' name. Amen

3|JUSTICE

God invites us to be part of the mission of justice.

COME AS YOU ARE

When Paul told the Christians in Galatia that God had set them free for a life of doing what God wants (remember Session 2?), this wasn't an entirely new concept. More than 700 years before Jesus was even born, God sent a message through the prophet Micah telling the people of Israel exactly what that kind of life looked like. It isn't that these people weren't "religious." They thought they knew what God wanted. They *wanted* to do what God wanted *and* they thought they were doing it. They were wrong. God is on a mission to create a just and fair world. And God wants us to help make that happen.

Check in with each other before you get to work. Talk about what's been happening in your life over the past couple of weeks and whether this No Experience Necessary Bible study has been making a difference for you. Next, pray together, with someone new taking a turn at offering a free-form prayer. Then, if you choose, you can pray this prayer together:

Holy God, we want to live life the way you want us to. Help us hear you speaking to us as we study the Bible together. Teach us how to live. In Jesus' name. Amen

JUST **3** QUESTIONS

Open your Bibles to Micah 6:1-8. Take turns reading this passage, a verse or two at a time, out loud. Then spend some time talking about what is happening in this passage, including what you are hearing God say here. Use these three questions as a starting point to have this conversation:

1 | What do you think God is doing here?

2 | What do you hear God saying to you, personally?

3 | What do you hear God saying to us (as a small group, congregation, community, nation)?

GROUP TIPS

COME AS YOU ARE

It is important to check in with each other, on a personal level, before you begin studying. For some groups, this will be easier than others. In fact, some groups might have to be careful not to spend TOO MUCH time doing this. If you're in a group that likes to chat, don't be afraid to gently remind everyone that there is work to be done. God has something to say to you during this session! Get to it.

JUST 3 QUESTIONS

These 3 questions are meant to be discussion starters, not stoppers. If someone seems to be taking a detour (talking about his or her view on a passage or an issue, for example) you might want to let him or her go for a little while. Some of the most interesting conversations happen as you follow paths you weren't expecting. You can help keep the conversation positive and helpful, though, by remembering to ask the MAIN question: "Okay, so what do you see God doing—or hear God saying—here?"

What does God want?

GROUP TIPS

HEART OF THE MATTER

Give each other time to quietly read the "Heart of the Matter" article titled "What Does God Want?" (unless you all agreed to read it during the past week). Then take a few minutes to talk about it. Use the discussion questions at the end of the article to get you going.

Religion exists to help us answer some really important questions: What does God want *from* us? What does God want *for* us? And what does God want for the world? The problem is that "religion" includes fallen human beings. And fallen human beings—by definition!—tend to make a mess of things.

One of the mistakes we make is to think about "what God wants" in terms of what we are already doing. And when religion only gives us one answer to the question "What does God want from us?" no matter what that one answer is, we are probably wrong.

That was exactly the situation about the year 715 B.C. This was a long time before Jesus was born, at a time when the people of God were living as a nation, called Israel, under a king. And, as happens whenever a bunch of people live together, some of the powerful were abusing their power. But here is the strange thing: When people back then asked, "What does God want?" they didn't think about how the powerful were sticking it to those with less power. They didn't think, "Maybe God wants us to do something about that!" Instead, they thought of...worship! Their religion said, "God wants us to worship. God wants us to bring flour, olive oil, and animals as offerings for worship. That is what God wants."

> What does God want *from* us? What does God want *for* us? And what does God want for the world?

An important message

Enter stage right: the messenger *Micah*. Flowing robes, sandals, long beard, angry look on his face. God had spoken to Micah. Now Micah brought God's message to the people. (Warning: Be prepared—the message wasn't pretty.)

First, through Micah, God asked the people this question: "What have I done to you that you have grown tired of listening to me? Oh, I know what I did! *I saved you from Egypt!* I sent you Moses and Miriam to be your leaders! I brought you out of slavery! I gave you the promised land to live in! You must think that I am a *really bad Lord!* That must be why you quit following the commandments that I gave for you!"

God sends us
out to speak up
for those who
are getting
stepped on by
those in power.

Then Micah reported what God did and did not want: "Do you really think that God wants you to worship? Why would God want that?!? Do you think God would be happy if you brought God a baby cow? No? How about 1,000 rams? No? How about 10,000 RIVERS OF OIL? NO? THEN HOW ABOUT IF YOU KILLED YOUR FIRSTBORN CHILD, DOES GOD WANT THAT?!?" (Now this might sound crazy, but some people in ancient Israel did, in fact, believe that sacri-ficing a son made God happy. We are not making this up.)

Finally, Micah ended God's mes-sage: "What God wants is for you to do justice, to love mercy, and to walk humbly with God." *This*—and not all that other crazy stuff—is what God wants from you.

What is justice?

Micah wasn't saying that we shouldn't worship. Worship is a part of a relationship with God. But our relationship with God should make a difference in our relationships with other people. God does not want us to over-look the world's problems. In fact, God wants us to be part of the solution.

God is on a mission to create a just and fair world. And God calls us to be a part of that mission. God sends us out to speak up for those who are getting *stepped on* by those in power...political power, economic power, social power, military power, even religious power.

God says: "Do justice. Love mercy. Walk humbly with God."

Who are the people who get "stepped on" in our time? How could we speak up for them? How can we help create a just and fair world today?

The real issue

I n many churches in the United States today, Christians have this idea that what God wants from us is a "cleaned-up" private life. (And mostly what that means is a cleaned-up sex life.) We spend a lot of time, in fact, arguing about what that looks like. But Micah seemed to have other things on his mind.

So did Jesus. *Read Matthew 23:23* for a glimpse into the kinds of things Jesus cared about.

Jesus is on a rampage against the "scribes and Pharisees," the religious leaders in his time. Jesus doesn't have

"What God really wants," Jesus says, "is for you to practice *justice* and mercy and faith."

much to say about their sex lives but, wow, does he have other issues with them: "You're a bunch of hypocrites!" he shouts. "You think just because you're giving a measly 10 percent (and it was measly too—mint, dill, and cumin were the tiniest herbs they could find!), you're right with God. Well, think again! God isn't fooled by your 'holier-than-thou' attitude. God can see the way you are treating other people, the way you exclude and abuse them. *You lock people out of the kingdom of heaven*" (Matthew 23:13)!!!!

"What God really wants," Jesus says, "is for you to practice *justice* and mercy and faith."

What does he mean? Let's look at how these words are used in Matthew's Gospel: *Faith* isn't about "accepting Jesus"; it means believing that, with God, nothing is impossible (21:18-22). *Mercy* means putting the needs of others first, even before "the rules" (9:13; 12:7) and practicing forgiveness (18:23-25). And *justice*...well, the only other place that word appears is in a quote from the prophet Isaiah (12:18, 20), for whom justice was (like in Micah) looking out for the powerless.

It would be going too far to say Jesus didn't care about what people did in their private lives. God cares about ALL of life. But when the Bible talks about God's *judgment*, it talks about it in the context of *justice*. The strongest thing Jesus has to say about judgment, in fact, comes in 25:31-46. It is all about the way we care for those who are hungry, strangers, poor, sick, and those in prison.

There are probably a few new conversations we ought to be having together, don't you think?

In your opinion, why do so many Christians today tend to make the "private" aspects of faith more important than the "public" ones? What do you think Jesus would say about that?

GROUP TIPS

After you've finished talking about the "Heart of the Matter" article, browse through the rest of the session. Pick one or two additional articles from "Another Look," "Right to the Point," "Bible Basics," or "Right Here, Right Now." Read these articles out loud or silently. Then talk about them. Use the discussion questions to spark your conversation.

You most likely will not get through all of the articles, so pick the ones your group is most interested in. Encourage group members to read the rest of the articles on their own during the week.

ANOTHER LOOK

"Another Look" explores this session's theme from the perspective of another book in the Bible.

Have someone who is willing read Matthew 23:23.

Cut from the same cloth

So who was Micah, exactly? Read Micah 1:1 to find out a little about him. Okay, maybe that didn't help much. Here's some more: Micah lived about the same time as the prophet Isaiah. (Check out Isaiah 1:1. The same kings are listed there.) And he came from a place called Moresheth. Never heard of it? Well, it's not there anymore. And it wasn't much of a place even back then. It was a rural area, a good couple days' walk from Jerusalem. The city people in Jerusalem probably would have thought of Micah as a "hick."

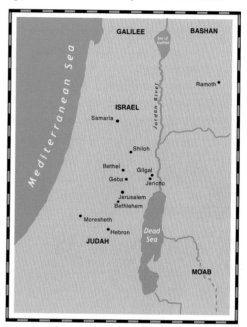

Frankly, though, the same thing could have been said about Jesus. Seven hundred years later, he was born in a little town called Bethlehem, about a day's walk closer to Jerusalem than Moresheth but still in the middle of nowhere. Weirdly enough, Micah seems to predict this (Micah 5:1-5). At least that's what early Christians thought when they reread these words: "But you, O Bethlehem of Ephrathah, who are one of the little clans of Judah, from you shall come forth for me one who is to rule in Israel, whose origin is from of old, from ancient days" (Micah 5:2). It's hard to know exactly what Micah meant by this, but it's hard *not* to see Jesus in it.

Anyway, the point is that God seems to have this habit of sending messages with people who were cut from the same cloth. Namely, they are people who seem to come out of *nowhere*. God, in fact, seems to love taking people who are *nobodies* and making something out of them. David was a shepherd from the least important family in his nation before he became the king of Israel. Mary was a pregnant teenager with nothing when she became the most blessed among all women.

This is God's way, perhaps, of reminding us that people who are poor and powerless matter. No wonder God gets so angry when they are treated unfairly, ignored, taken advantage of, excluded. In fact, in Micah, it's the elite—who make all the decisions and cause trouble for the little guys—who are in the doghouse, as far as God is concerned. God loves all the "nobodies" out there and lifts them up and sees something in them that others have a hard time seeing.

The Bible says the word of the Lord came to Micah. We should be very careful about how we treat a guy like that.

God loves people who are poor and powerless. How is that good news for you?

> God loves all the "nobodies" out there and lifts them up and sees something in them that others have a hard time seeing.

Take the extra step

ustice is a big word and a broad concept. Couldn't *justice* mean just about anything that a person wants it to mean? Yes, and that is exactly the problem!

When readers of the Bible come up against a broad concept such as *justice*, they risk treating the word like a movie screen and then projecting their own ideas onto the word. How can we avoid that? How do we decide what *justice* means? More to the point, if Micah calls us to join God's mission of justice, what things should we do and what things should we not do?

A key way to get at questions like these is to read the word or passage we are wondering about *in context*. If we want to know what Micah means by *justice*, for example, the first thing we'll do is look up other passages where Micah talks about it. Then we'll read these passages and learn from them. We'll resist even talking about the word without first learning how the author used it in other places!

This "extra step" helps us avoid projecting so much of our own self onto the word.

When we look at the rest of the book of Micah, here are some examples of behavior we find Micah condemning:

- "They covet fields, and seize them" (2:2).
- "The women of my people you drive out from their pleasant houses" (2:9).
- "[You] cry 'Peace'...but declare war against those who put nothing into their mouths" (3:5).
- "Its rulers give judgment for a bribe, its priests teach for a price, its prophets give oracles for money" (3:11).
- "Can I tolerate wicked scales and a bag of dishonest weights?" (6:11).

From these passages it is clear that Micah is condemning unethical business practices, corruption in the legal and religious circles, people going hungry and being driven from their homes, and the dishonest seizure of property.

God calls us to avoid actions such as these. Working for justice means working toward a world where those who are hungry are fed, where all of life is protected, where all property is protected, and where integrity and fairness are part of business, church, and public life.

How would you have defined *justice* before taking the *extra step*? Why is it important not to project ourselves onto the words we read in the Bible?

DO NOT

READ WORD

DISCUSS MEANING

DO

READ WORD

LEARN FROM CONTEXT

DISCUSS MEANING

GROUP TIPS

RIGHT TO THE POINT

"Right to the Point" goes deeper into this session's theme or explores it from a different angle.

Have someone read Micah 1:1.

BIBLE BASICS

"Bible Basics" will help you learn more about how to read and understand the Bible.

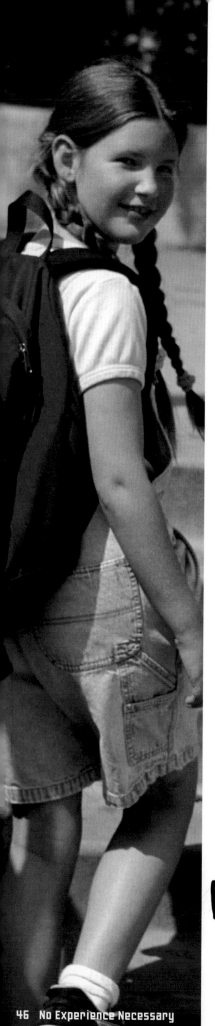

Kelly A. Fryer

I see you

My daughter was 10 years old when we visited Washington, D.C., for the first time. This is a place where it is easy to get overwhelmed by the BIGNESS of everything. The buildings are big. The people are big. The significance of every monument, every memorialized event is big.

But it was something definitely NOT big that caught her eye.

A couple of guys who were homeless hung out on the street right outside our hotel every day. She asked us if she could give them the money she had saved and brought along for souvenirs. We explained that we give away a lot of money to support organizations (like Bread for the World, Lutheran World Relief, and the Heifer Project) that help people like this and that, as hard as it sounds, giving actual *money* to people on the street might not really help them. They need a different kind of help, we said. But they're probably hungry, she said. But they might spend their money on bad things, we said, instead of food.

Right or wrong, this argument did not deter my daughter.

Every morning at breakfast, she filled her pockets and her little backpack with granola bars and apples and whatever else she could carry away from the buffet. And she was her own little food pantry all day long. She looked at the people when she gave them food. She smiled at them, a brave kind of smile that said, "Don't for a minute think that you don't matter. Because you do." She didn't do this because she felt sorry for the people she met on the street. She did it because she knew it was *wrong* that they were hungry. And she was determined to do whatever she could to change that.

Imagine what the world would be like if we were all that determined.

What do you wish you or your congregation could help change? What are you going to do about it?

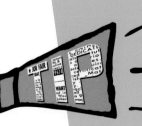

The Hebrew word *mishpat* means both "justice" (the abstract concept) and also "judgment" (the concrete decision). One of the things we can learn from this is that there is no absolute division between theory and practice. A theory—such as justice—must be embodied in actual practice. And practice—such as making judgments—must always be informed by theory.

Wrap up

When all we have is a hammer, everything looks like a nail. Religion is always in dangerous territory when it claims to have the one right answer, no matter what that answer is. The prophet Micah warned the people of Israel that what God wanted from them was not what they thought God wanted at all. God wanted them to help create a fair and just world for everyone, especially for the powerless and the poor. For next time, read Mark 16:1-8 and come prepared to think together about another aspect of God's mission in the world: Reconciliation.

What can you do to help bring more justice and fairness into the places where you work and live this week?

Before you go, pray together. Try to have someone new pray this time. This prayer doesn't have to be fancy. Just a simple prayer thanking God for being with you as you studied together would be fine. At the end, pray the Lord's Prayer together out loud:

Our Father in heaven,
Hallowed be your name,
Your kingdom come,
Your will be done,
On earth as in heaven.
Give us today our daily bread.
Forgive us our sins
As we forgive those who sin against us.
Save us from the time of trial
And deliver us from evil.
For the kingdom, the power,
And the glory are yours,
Now and forever. Amen

GROUP TIPS

RIGHT HERE, RIGHT NOW

"Right Here, Right Now" connects this session's theme with real life.

GET GOING

Read "Wrap Up" out loud or silently. Then take turns answering the question.

Agree to "homework" for the coming week. Also consider reading chapter 3 in the book *No Experience Necessary: Everybody's Welcome*, if you haven't already done this.

End by praying together. If your group is comfortable with prayer, you can be creative and do your own thing. Be careful, though, not to have just one or two people turn into the prayer "experts." Some people may be more hesitant or shy about it, but still willing. Remember: Everyone has something to offer.

God invites us to be part of the mission of reconciliation.

4|RECONCILIATIO

COME as YOU aRE

God has a special concern for those who are poor and power-less (see Session 3!), but no one is beyond God's care and concern. God wants to be in a relationship with every single one of us, no matter who we are or what we've done. There is, perhaps, no better picture of this than the one we find in our main Bible reading for this session. Here we read, from the very end of Mark's Gospel, the story of the first Easter Day. Jesus, who had been killed and buried, has now been raised from the dead. And the first thing God does is reach out to bring Jesus back together with those who had deserted and denied him. That is just who God is. God is on a mission to bring reconciliation to the whole world. And we are called to be a part of it.

Spend time checking in with each other. Talk about how your week has gone. Then take time to pray. Hopefully, people in your group have been taking turns doing this. If you volunteer to pray, be sure to ask God to be present with you as you study. Invite the Holy Spirit to fill your conversation. Thank God for your group! When you're done, if it's still helpful to use a written prayer together, pray this out loud:

Loving God, there is no one beyond your concern. Thank you for caring about us even when we do not deserve it. Teach us more about this during our study time. Help us learn from each other. In Jesus' name. Amen

JUST **3** QUESTIONS

Open your Bibles to Mark 16:1-8. Take turns reading this passage, a verse or two at a time, out loud. Then spend some time talking about what is happening in this passage, including what you are hearing God say here. Use these three questions as a starting point to have this conversation:

1| What do you think God is doing here?

2| What do you hear God saying to you, personally?

3| What do you hear God saying to us (as a small group, congregation, community, nation)?

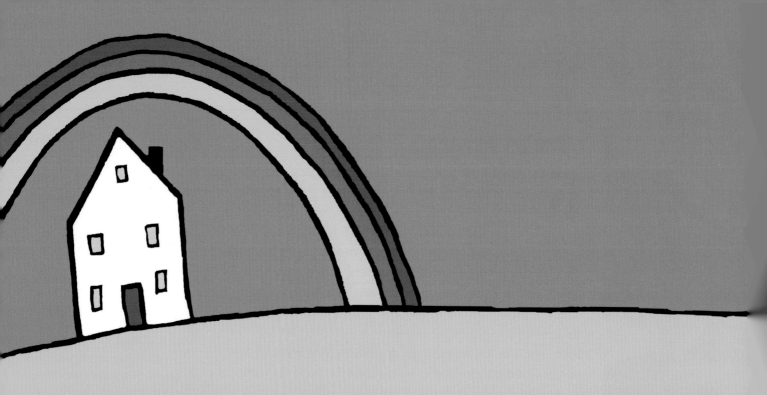

A powerful picture

The Bible uses many metaphors and images to describe how human beings are separated from God. Maybe the most powerful is when the Bible describes us as "sojourners," "foreigners," and "strangers." The idea here is that earth is not our permanent home and that, while we are here, we are temporarily separated from *our true home*, which is with God. The promise of the gospel is that God has prepared a permanent home for us where we will be with God in a permanent way. In other words, God is on a mission to reconcile the differences between us and God...and bring us all back home again. There are few more powerful pictures of what this looks like than in our reading from Mark 16:1-8.

> God is on a mission to reconcile the differences between us and God.

Three terrible statements

Jesus called disciples to follow him. He taught the disciples and sent them out to share in his mission to the world. One of the main disciples was Peter. Peter was the first to call Jesus the Messiah (8:27-29). And Peter was the one who promised Jesus that he would never abandon him, even if Jesus got hauled off to die (14:29).

But when the soldiers arrested Jesus and Jesus was put on trial, Peter blew it big time. He was asked three times if he knew who Jesus was. And three times Peter stated, "Nope, not me. You have me confused with someone else. Never met him" (14:54-72).

In the Gospel of Mark, those are the last words Peter speaks.

Two wonderful words

Pick up the story, now, on the first Easter morning. God has raised Jesus from the dead. An angel has appeared to Mary Magdalene, Mary the mother of James, and Salome. And here's the angel's message: "Go, tell his disciples and Peter that [Jesus] is going ahead of you to Galilee; there you will see him, just as he told you" (16:7).

We are sent to tell all the world that God's love is stronger than hate and sin and death combined.

Did you catch those two little words: *and Peter*?! Peter had to be singled out because, when Peter said three times he didn't know Jesus, he removed himself from being a disciple! With his own last words, Peter had separated himself from Jesus.

But Jesus does not let us have the last word.

When it comes to God's relationship with us, God always promises to have the last word. Jesus cannot let us sever our relationship with him. He cannot allow the dead to remain dead or sinners to remain unforgiven. So even when we become strangers to God, God keeps being a friend to us. Even when we run away from God, God keeps chasing us and welcoming us back home. Even when we are not reconciled to God, God makes things right between us.

A word to share

But what about those women the angel spoke to? Notice that the young man at the tomb did not appear directly to Peter to deliver God's message of reconciliation. No, but he had a job for the women. *They* were supposed to bring God's message to Peter. To put it another way, God had a *mission* for them. Their mission was to tell Peter—and the world—about God's mission.

For that reason, Mary Magdalene is often called "the first apostle." In Greek, the word *apostle* means "one who is sent." God sent Mary Magdalene and the other women to bring the mission of reconciliation to Peter.

God sends us with the same message. We are sent to tell all the world that God's love is stronger than hate and sin and death combined. We are sent out to bring God's mission of reconciliation to the world.

The Bible also uses many metaphors and images to describe what it means for us to be sent out on this mission. Maybe the most powerful is when the Bible calls us "ambassadors." We are sent out to tell all of the other "sojourners," "foreigners," and "strangers" out there that God is near and God's love is pure and God wants—more than anything—for them to be brought back home again.

Does someone in your life need to hear this special word from God? How can you share it? What is a helpful way to share God's good news? What isn't helpful?

Act like it

The apostle Paul spent a lot of time talking about God's mission of reconciliation because Paul spent a lot of time talking to people who needed this message. He had a foot in two camps, so to speak. He was a Jew by birth. But he was called to take the good news to the Gentiles (everybody who wasn't Jewish). And there were big differences between these two groups.

Read a bit from his letter to the Christians in Ephesus to get a sense of how Paul approached this issue. Go ahead and *read Ephesians 2:11-14* right now.

First, Paul acknowledged the problem. He didn't try to cover it up or pretend it wasn't there. "We are really different from each other!" he said. "We are aliens to each other and strangers. There is hostility between us."

Second, he announced that Christ has broken down the walls that divide people. He didn't say this *might* happen. He said this HAS happened. "Christ is our peace!" he said. "In his flesh he has made both groups into one." In other words, Paul said, when Christ died he died for *everyone*. And that makes us ONE people. When we stand at the foot of the cross, we stand there together...shoulder to shoulder...each one just as guilty...and just as loved...as the other.

Reconciliation is a reality. It isn't a hope or a wish or a dream. It is REAL and it has already happened, through Jesus Christ.

Our only job now is to LIVE INTO that new reality. Our call is to look across the rubble of the dividing wall and recognize— even in our worst enemy—the face of someone Christ died for.

"You are no longer strangers and aliens," Paul said, "but you are citizens with the saints and also members of the household of God" (Ephesians 2:19). All the walls have been knocked down. All the lines have been erased. You are family now.

Act like it.

What would it be like if, in your congregation, workplace, neighborhood, or home, people acted like they were all members of God's household?

GROUP TIPS

After you've finished talking about the "Heart of the Matter" article, browse through the rest of the session. Pick one or two additional articles from "Another Look," "Right to the Point," "Bible Basics," or "Right Here, Right Now." Read these articles out loud or silently. Then talk about them. Use the discussion questions to spark your conversation.

You most likely will not get through all of the articles, so pick the ones your group is most interested in. Encourage group members to read the rest of the articles on their own during the week.

ANOTHER LOOK

"Another Look" explores this session's theme from the perspective of another book in the Bible.

Take turns reading Ephesians 2:11-14.

For Jews at the time of Jesus, the word "Gentile" referred to everyone who was not Jewish. The word actually is related to the term for "nations," meaning theirs was the "Jewish Nation" and all others belonged simply to "the nations."

Awe-some

I n November 1977 Anwar Sadat, then President of Egypt, became the first Arab leader to visit Israel. He was determined, for the sake of generations to come, to make peace with this most bitter enemy. One of the first people to address him was Israel's former Prime Minister, Golda Meir. Mrs. Meir had ferociously led her nation through years of bitter violence, including war with Egypt. But she also hoped for peace.

The eyes of the world were on these two that day. People watched in awe as Mrs. Meir leaned toward President Sadat to give him a gift. "As a grandmother to a grandfather," she said, "may I give you a little present for your new granddaughter, and thank you for the present you have given me."

Awe is what people feel when they all of a sudden find themselves in the presence of something—or someone—holy. *Read Mark 4:35-41* right now to see how the disciples responded when they saw Jesus for who he really was. They were so afraid and they were awestruck, Mark says, because they saw the real power of Jesus when he commanded a storm to cease.

Likewise, the women at the tomb on that first Easter morning were filled with such "terror and amazement" that they ran away from the tomb and didn't tell anyone what they had seen (16:8). (We know that's not the end of the story, of course, because we now know about it!)

What we *don't* know is what created such awe in the women in the first place.

Was it really just an empty tomb and the appearance of a "young man, dressed in a white robe" (16:5)? Possibly. Or maybe they couldn't believe their ears: "Go tell his disciples and Peter" (16:7)?! The women knew what those guys had done. They had deserted Jesus when he needed them most. And Peter was the worst of all. "God wants us to go tell those guys?!? Those guys should BE here right now. (Notice that they aren't!) Can God's heart really be that big?"

The amazing, awe-inspiring answer is, "Yes." God's heart *is* that big. It's big enough to embrace the fiercest enemy, the ugliest opponent, the most cowardly deserter. It is big enough to embrace even you and me, and enable us to embrace others.

Have you ever seen—or experienced—real reconciliation between people? Would you describe it as a holy thing? Why or why not?

God's heart *is* that big. It's big enough to embrace the fiercest enemy, the ugliest opponent, the most cowardly deserter.

Storytelling 101

GROUP TIPS

There are four Gospels in the New Testament: Matthew, Mark, Luke, and John. Each of these Gospels tells the story of Jesus. Each tells about the same Jesus. Each tells how he was crucified and raised for you and for me. The four have many similarities.

But the four Gospels also have some differences. Mark (the earliest written Gospel) starts with Jesus as an adult. Matthew starts with the birth of

Each Gospel writer was telling the story of Jesus to a different audience, in a different place, at a slightly different time.

Jesus. Luke starts with the birth of Jesus' cousin, John the Baptist. The Gospel of John starts out with philosophy, talking about Jesus as "the Word."

The four Gospels also end differently. Mark originally ended at 16:8, with the women running away afraid. (Other endings were added later, perhaps because the sudden ending made audiences uncomfortable.) Matthew ends with Jesus promising always to be with the disciples as they go out to spread the gospel. Luke ends with the

disciples praising God in the temple. And John ends by noting that if everything Jesus did were written down, the entire world could not contain all the books that would be necessary.

Why are there differences between the four Gospels? Because each Gospel writer was telling the story of Jesus to a different audience, in a different place, at a slightly different time.

My family is full of storytellers. There is a funny thing about good storytellers—every time they tell a story, the story is a little bit different. Why? Because they tailor the story to fit the audience at that particular time. I have heard my father tell one story a dozen different ways, each slightly altered to fit the audience.

Does this mean that only one of the stories is true? NO! It is just that when a storyteller chooses which details to include in a story, the storyteller is thinking about what point he or she is trying to make. So each Gospel writer chose a different place to start and to end and different details to include in the story because their points were slightly different.

When we read, we listen for the point that the storyteller is making.

If somebody asked you to tell the story of Jesus, in a nutshell, what would you say? How would you say it to really get across who Jesus is to you?

RIGHT TO THE POINT

"Right to the Point" goes deeper into this session's theme or explores it from a different angle.

Take turns reading Mark 4:35-41.

BIBLE BASICS

"Bible Basics" will help you learn more about how to read and understand the Bible.

Rolf A. Jacobson

Friends

> We pass the peace as a sign that we are reconciled to one another through Christ. We reconcile with one another because Christ was first reconciled to us.

When I was in ninth grade, I got into a tiff with one of my friends. We shared interests such as sports and other hobbies. We went to the same church, so we also spent time together at summer Bible camps. But for some reason, we had a falling out.

I still can't remember what started the spat—but since I know myself pretty well, I have to assume that it was 99.5 percent my fault. I also cannot remember how long the spat lasted.

But I recall perfectly the exact moment when reconciliation happened.

I went to worship one Sunday morning, as I always did. On this particular Sunday, my older sister and I decided to sit together. She was aware of the falling out I had experienced with my friend. The pews were starting to fill up, so we quickly found two spots along the aisle, about halfway up, on the right side.

A minute later, my friend and his parents slipped into the pew in front of us. He did not turn to say hello. I didn't mind.

The sermon that morning was about making peace with our neighbors. About forgiving one another because Christ had first forgiven us, about being reconciled to each other because through Christ we had been reconciled to God.

When the pastor said "Amen" and sat down, I leaned over to my sister

and whispered, "I hope he was listening to that sermon." She knew who I meant by "he." She whispered back into my ear, "I hope you were listening."

Big sisters are like that sometimes.

A few minutes later came the time in the service when the congregation was to "pass the peace." Passing the peace is not about saying good morning to each other. We pass the peace as a sign that we are reconciled to one another through Christ. We reconcile with one another because Christ was first reconciled to us.

He turned around, stuck out his hand and said, "The peace of the Lord be with you." I grabbed his hand and replied, "And also with you."

The next day in school, we were friends again.

Is there somebody in your life you need to be reconciled with? What could you do to make the first move?

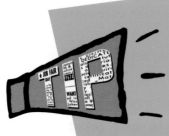

In order to get across the great truths about God, the Bible often uses metaphors. The Bible speaks of God as shepherd, potter, rock, host of a banquet, light, property owner, and so on. Likewise, human beings are described as pottery, sojourners, strangers, sheep and so on. Each metaphor offers a peek into one part of how God relates to us.

Wrap up

God is on a mission of reconciliation, bringing the whole world back home again. In fact, the first thing that happened after Jesus was killed, buried, and raised from the dead on Easter was that God reached out with reconciliation to those who had deserted and denied Jesus. In Christ, all the things that separate us from God and from each other have been destroyed. We are reconciled people! Our call is to share this good news with everyone...and to live, every day, like it's real. For next time, read about God's mission of love in John 13:1-35.

What will you do differently during the coming week as a result of something you heard or thought or experienced during this session?

RIGHT HERE, RIGHT NOW

"Right Here, Right Now" connects this session's theme with real life.

GET GOING

Read "Wrap Up" out loud or silently. Then take turns answering the question.

Agree to any "homework" for the coming week. As a group, also consider reading chapter 4 in the book *No Experience Necessary: Everybody's Welcome*.

End by praying together, preferably taking turns. Don't push it, though, if people are still really uncomfortable with this. Be kind and encourage each other gently. Give members of your group space to come to God in their own time and way. If you do decide to take turns, be sure everyone knows she or he can opt out and just pray silently.

Pray before you go. Since you've been meeting for several sessions now, try going around the circle and take turns praying. Make it simple. Say thanks for the session. Ask for help with something you're facing during the week. When it's your turn, if you're uncomfortable praying out loud, just pray silently, and, when you're done, say "Amen" so the next person knows when to start. When everyone has had a turn, pray the Lord's Prayer together out loud:

Our Father in heaven,
Hallowed be your name,
Your kingdom come,
Your will be done,
On earth as in heaven.
Give us today our daily bread.
Forgive us our sins
As we forgive those who sin against us.
Save us from the time of trial
And deliver us from evil.
For the kingdom, the power,
And the glory are yours,
Now and forever. Amen

God invites us to be part of the mission of love.

5 | LOVE

COME AS YOU ARE

God is on a mission to re-create and reconcile the whole world, to see justice done, to bring freedom to all people. Why? It's simple: God loves us. Furthermore, God loves everyone. And God wants us to love one another. Unlike the kind of love we often see advertised in our culture, however, the love we are talking about here is anything but mushy. It isn't even really a feeling. It is an action. It is radical and self-giving. It is the kind of love that leads, sometimes, even to the cross.

Check in with each other before you get going. Then pray together. If possible, have someone new lead the prayer this time. This doesn't have to be hard or scary. Just ask God to be with your group as you study. When you're done, if it's still helpful to use a written prayer, pray this out loud together:

Thank you, God, for loving us. Teach us to love each other. And let our love for each other spill over into your world, to touch the lives of everyone we meet. In Jesus' name. Amen

JUST 3 QUESTIONS

Open your Bibles to John 13:1-35. Take turns reading this passage, a verse or two at a time, out loud. Then spend some time talking about what is happening in this passage, including what you are hearing God say here. Use these three questions as a starting point to have this conversation:

1 | **What do you think God is doing here?**

2 | **What do you hear God saying to you, personally?**

3 | **What do you hear God saying to us (as a small group, congregation, community, nation)?**

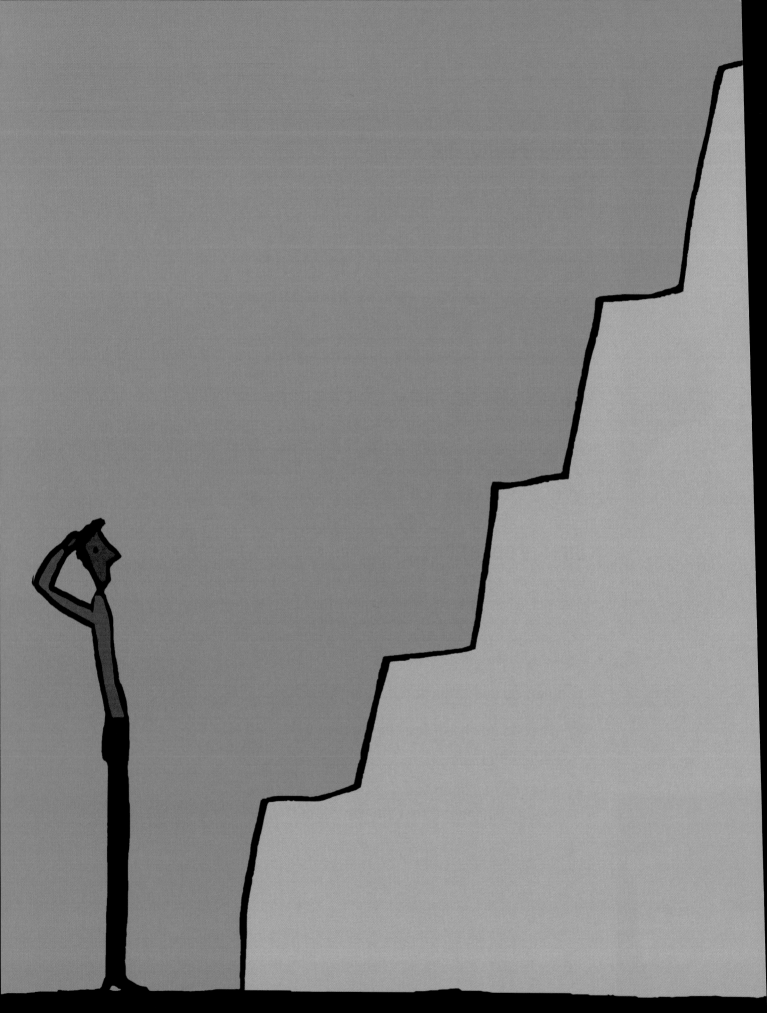

It's this simple

The Gospel of John is one of four Gospels in the New Testament. Unfortunately, biblical authors didn't put a date and time stamp on their documents before e-mailing them to their publishers! However, using clues given in the text itself, scholars have been able to guess that John's Gospel was the last to be written.

You don't have to be an expert, though, to notice that this Gospel uses more symbolic language than the others when it comes to talking about Jesus Christ. This author was part of a faith community that used wonderfully symbolic—even poetic—language to talk about who Jesus was and what his coming meant for the world. It is here in John's Gospel that Jesus is described as "the bread of life" (John 6:35), "the good shepherd" (10:11), "the way, and the truth, and the life" (14:6), and "the true vine" (15:1). It's sort of ironic, therefore, that when it comes to describing the mission Jesus was on, John's Gospel says it in the most down-to-earth way possible:

Jesus came to earth because God loves us
(see John 3:16).

It doesn't get much simpler than that.

Down and dirty

God is on a mission to love the whole world. This may be simple, but it is not what you would call warm and fuzzy. Not even close. God's love is down and dirty.

> We could never somehow make our way "up" to God. God's love *always* comes down.

Picture Jesus, knowing the end is near, getting down on bended knee to wash the dusty feet of the people who were about to desert and deny him. Peter resisted when Jesus came near. "No way, Jesus! I should be washing YOUR feet...not the other way around!" And we don't know what Judas (the one who set Jesus up to be arrested) was thinking as he felt the strong hands of his Lord washing his feet, performing a servant's task, loving him in spite of what he was about to do.

God's love doesn't come only to those who deserve it—which is a good thing because none of us really do. The truth is none of us could ever earn God's love.

GROUP TIPS

HEART OF THE MATTER

Give each other time to quietly read the "Heart of the Matter" article titled "It's This Simple" (unless you all agreed to read it during the past week). Then take a few minutes to talk about it. Use the discussion questions at the end of the article to get you going.

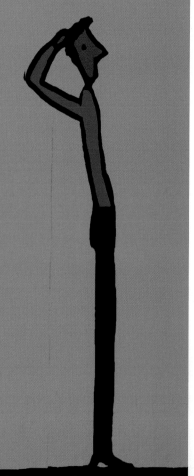

God's love has come to us and that love sets us free to love others.

We could never somehow make our way "up" to God. God's love *always* comes down. It comes down to people who are sinful and broken and lost, even to the most unlovable and undeserving of all. It comes to people like Judas...and me...and you.

Love in action

There is enormous power in a love like this. It changes people. It shaped the life of Jesus himself. The Gospel writer tells us Jesus knew how deeply he was loved by God. He knew "the Father had given all things into his hands, and that he had come from God and was going to God" (13:3). He knew that nothing could ever separate him from God. Knowing these things, Jesus got up from the table, took off his outer robe, tied a towel around himself...and began to wash his disciples' feet.

Jesus gave us a commandment to love one another. But he didn't leave it at that. He showed us love in action.

He washed feet. He carried a cross. He gave his life away for us, even though we didn't deserve it. And he loved us as he did it. In all this, we have been loved beyond all expectation and beyond all reason. We have been literally loved to death.

Being loved the way God loves us makes us able to love others like that. We choose to love even when it's difficult, even when we don't feel like it. It's not easy! But we choose to love because God's love has come to us and that love sets us free to love others.

Love each other the way I have loved you, Jesus said. (See 15:12.)

Really now. Did he even have to *say* it?

What difference does it make to know that you are loved by God? Does it make it any easier to love others?

ANOTHER LOOK

A strange way to say it

G od's prophets pretty much did anything they could to get God's messages across. Isaiah walked around the city naked. Jeremiah wore an ox's harness. Ezekiel ate a scroll, and so on. But perhaps Hosea, on God's orders, went the furthest.

God told Hosea to marry Gomer, who was what one translation calls a "wife of whoredom." Scholars don't agree on what this term means. Some think it means she was a prostitute; others think she was a sexually unfaithful woman. And there are other views. But one thing is clear: She was not faithful to Hosea.

But no matter how many times Gomer cheated on Hosea, no matter how many times she ran off after other lovers, no matter how unfaithful she was, Hosea kept loving her. He kept calling her to return to him. He kept begging her to return his love.

The point of Hosea's action was this: God loves us. God is on a mission to love us no matter what we do. We are all—some more, others less, but all—*unfaithful* to God. But God's love is permanent.

Hosea and Gomer had children. Hosea gave them funny names. In Hebrew, the names of the last two children meant "Not Shown Mercy" and "Not My People." Hosea's point was that because the people had left

God, they had put themselves in a position in which they no longer deserved God's mercy and they no longer deserved to be God's people.

But that was not the end of the story. Right now, *read Hosea 11:1-9.* Pay special attention to verses 8-9. Notice how God is like a father or mother who has rebellious children, but loves them anyway.

We are God's children. God loves us so fiercely, so completely, that God will never let us go. And for that reason, we are free (do you remember Session 2?) to love each other with the same passion and loyalty. Just as Hosea always loved Gomer and begged her to return his love, we are free to love each other. Just as a mother loves her children, even when they break her heart, so we are free to love all of God's hurting world.

> We are God's children. God loves us so fiercely, so completely, that God will never let us go.

What helps you continue to act in love toward someone, no matter how hard it gets?

GROUP TIPS

After you've finished talking about the "Heart of the Matter" article, browse through the rest of the session. Pick one or two additional articles from "Another Look," "Right to the Point," "Bible Basics," or "Right Here, Right Now." Read these articles out loud or silently. Then talk about them. Use the discussion questions to spark your conversation.

You most likely will not get through all of the articles, so pick the ones your group is most interested in. Encourage group members to read the rest of the articles on their own during the week.

ANOTHER LOOK

"Another Look" explores this session's theme from the perspective of another book in the Bible.

Have everyone who is willing take turns reading Hosea 11:1-9.

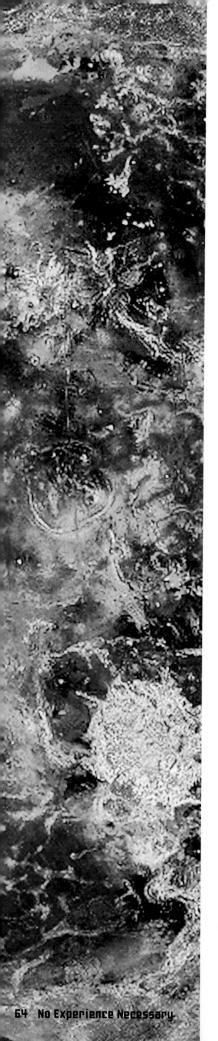

For the sake of the world

The way the stories are told in the Gospels of Matthew, Mark, and Luke, the last thing Jesus does in his ministry is to send his disciples out into the world with good news. Remember, we already looked at the ending of Mark. (See Session 4.) *Check out Matthew 28:16-20 and Luke 24:44-49. Now compare these endings to John 21:15-25.*

John's Gospel doesn't end anything like the others. Instead, Jesus tells Peter to "feed my sheep." And "my sheep" are those who "follow" him (John 10:4). In fact, readers of John's Gospel have noticed a certain inward focus throughout the story. Remember, for example, how the disciples are told to love "one another" in chapter 13.

In fact, Jesus loves his followers very much and he knows that following him is not always easy. He encourages them to stand firm in the face of suffering and persecution (15:18–16:4). He prays that they will stay unified no matter how difficult things become (17:1-11). He reminds them to love each other, even if it means dying for one another (15:12-13). Jesus wants his community—the church—to be strong and healthy and vital. Why?

Because we have work to do.

Jesus' ministry, again and again, took him into all kinds of new places and into the company of strangers.

> **Following Jesus means following him into the world, as scary and as dangerous as that might sometimes be.**

Following Jesus means following him into the world, as scary and as dangerous as that might sometimes be. "For God so loved the world that he gave his only Son," John tells us (3:16). And just as the Father sent the Son, so we are sent out in the power of the Holy Spirit (20:21-22).

It would be a mistake to focus solely on the inward focus of John's Gospel and miss the clear outward focus. The truth is we are called to be the church—to love and look out for each other—*for the sake of the world*. In fact, this is the whole point of being the church.

The church is following Jesus into mission in and for the world...or it isn't the church at all.

What is your reaction to the idea that the church exists for the sake of people who aren't in it yet? How is the church being called to love?

What is love?

Most of us think that we know what love is. If you turn on the radio or the TV, you'll be bombarded with messages about love.

Most of those messages equate love as a feeling, as an emotion, as some warm and fuzzy, tingling sensation deep in your heart. Think about the saying "Love is blind." The whole idea is that feelings of love are so powerful they overwhelm your thinking so you do stupid things.

In the Bible, love is much, much, MUCH more than just an emotion. Love is a set of actions and inactions.

In the Bible, love is much, much, MUCH more than just an emotion. Love is a set of actions and inactions. Jesus says we are to love our neighbors as ourselves. This does not mean only that we are to think of, regard, or feel a certain way about our neighbors. Rather, when Jesus says to love our neighbor it means there are certain things we are TO DO and certain things that we are NOT TO DO.

In Romans 12:9, Paul writes, "Let love be genuine." Shortly after that, Paul names some specific behaviors for Christians to do and avoid doing. These are not things to do in addition to loving the neighbor. Doing these things is what it *means* to love the neighbor:

> "Contribute to the needs of the saints; extend hospitality to strangers. Bless those who persecute you; bless and do not curse them. Rejoice with those who rejoice, weep with those who weep. Live in harmony with one another; do not be haughty, but associate with the lowly; do not claim to be wiser than you are. Do not repay anyone evil for evil, but take thought for what is noble in the sight of all. If it is possible, so far as it depends on you, live peaceably with all" (12:13-18).

We could add a few things from our own lives. For starters, to love the neighbor means not cutting someone off on the freeway, not littering, picking up after others, paying your bills, showing up promptly at the time you promised, and so on.

In the Bible, love is more than a feeling. It is an action.

What things can we do or not do to love family members, friends, coworkers, neighbors, and strangers? What can we do or not do as a small group? As the church?

Kelly A. Fryer

The smell of love

I thought I had graduated from seminary equipped to go teach people something. Actually, I was the one who was taught. I learned my first lesson on my very first day as a pastor at the hospital where I met with a family from the congregation. All were distraught over the just-pronounced death of a loved one. He had been fighting cancer for a long time. But the end, even if expected, is never easy.

I struggled like the novice I was to find something, anything, to say. I left with a promise to show up later at their house and hoped I'd have thought of what to say by then. When I got there they were kind enough to open the door and let me in.

It was then that I was greeted by the smell of love.

You didn't know it had a smell, did you? Well, it does. It's the smell of freshly baked bread. Pie. Hamburger casserole. Meatballs. All of it delivered to the house by those who knew how to share the love that they themselves had received (excerpt from *No Experience Necessary: Everybody's Welcome*, Kelly A. Fryer, Augsburg Fortress, 2005, page 82).

I was greeted by the smell of love.

How would you describe love in the way we have been loved by God? What does it smell, sound, or look like?

In John 13:34, when Jesus says, "I give you a new commandment, that you love one another," the Greek word translated is *agape* (ah-gah-pay). By commanding us to love one another—our neighbors and even our enemies—Jesus isn't commanding us to have loving feelings but to do loving actions. And Jesus continues, "Just as I have loved you, you also should love one another."

Wrap up

God wants to save all the world, bringing in justice and rec-onciling people everywhere. God is on a wonderful mission to make all things new. Why? Because God is madly in love with this world and with every person in it. That changes the way we look at each other and ourselves. We are invited to love *as we have been loved*. That means loving others in a radical, self-giving way. It means taking ACTION on behalf and for the sake of our neighbors. For next week, read Luke 2:22-38 for another way of thinking about God's mission in the world: Salvation.

Who do you know who needs the kind of love God gives to us? How will you show this love this week?

Pray before you go. The last time you were together, you may have gone around the circle and taken turns praying, giving every-one an opportunity to pray either out loud or silently. If you didn't, try it now. When everyone has had a turn, pray the Lord's Prayer together out loud:

**Our Father in heaven,
Hallowed be your name,
Your kingdom come,
Your will be done,
On earth as in heaven.
Give us today our daily bread.
Forgive us our sins
As we forgive those who sin against us.
Save us from the time of trial
And deliver us from evil.
For the kingdom, the power,
And the glory are yours,
Now and forever. Amen**

GROUP TIPS

RIGHT HERE, RIGHT NOW

"Right Here, Right Now" connects this session's theme with real life.

GET GOING

Read "Wrap Up" out loud or silently. Then take turns answering the questions.

Agree to "homework" for the coming week. Consider reading chapter 4 in the book *No Experience Necessary: Everybody's Welcome* and talking about it next week.

End by praying together, preferably taking turns. Don't push it, though, if people are still uncomfortable with this. Encourage each other gently. Be kind and give members of the group space to come to God in their own time and their own way. If you do take turns, be sure everyone knows she or he can opt out and just pray silently.

God invites us to be part of
the mission of salvation.

6 | SALVATION

COME AS YOU ARE

Many Christians are used to the idea that God's mission is to *save*. Some Christians are even comfortable talking about the exact moment when they *got saved*. But salvation, in the Bible, is a much bigger concept than this. Simeon is an old man who SEES salvation come to him in the form of baby Jesus. Jesus is salvation, you might say, in the flesh. Through Jesus, we understand that salvation is both eternal—and right here, right now. It is personal—but it is also universal. It comes as a gift—but it is also a call. It changes everything.

Spend time catching up with each other and checking in. When you're done checking in, pray together. And if it's still helpful to use a written prayer, pray this out loud:

Lord Jesus, you are our life and our salvation. Help us to come to a deeper understanding of what that means. Make us eager to share it with everyone we know. Let it change us. In your name we pray. Amen

JUST 3 QUESTIONS

Open your Bibles to Luke 2:22-38. Take turns reading this passage, a verse or two at a time, out loud. Then spend some time talking about what is happening in this passage, including what you are hearing God say here. Use these three questions as a starting point to have this conversation:

1| **What do you think God is doing here?**

2| **What do you hear God saying to you, personally?**

3| **What do you hear God saying to us (as a small group, congregation, community, nation)?**

So much more

When Mary and Joseph brought Jesus into the temple, Simeon knew he was seeing something no one had ever seen before. He was seeing *salvation* in the flesh. Here was the one sent by God and set apart or anointed for this very purpose (anointed = Messiah = Christ!). Through Jesus, God would save Simeon, the people of Israel, and the whole world.

Simeon looked into the face of this child, an unlikely Savior, and did what only a very, very old man would have dared to do. Ignoring what must have been the startled expressions of the parents, Simeon took baby Jesus into his arms. And, filled with the power of the Holy Spirit, he praised God.

> Salvation through Jesus Christ means that we can face death with confidence, knowing that we have *eternal* life.

Peace at the last

Simeon's prayer began by thanking God for dismissing him "in peace" (Luke 2:29). He had been waiting for who knows how long, visiting the temple each day, hoping to finally see the Messiah. Now at last old Simeon was set free to die a good death.

Little did he know *how* good that death could be. Salvation through Jesus Christ means that we can face death with confidence, knowing that we have *eternal life*. To be sure, that baby grew up to carry a cross. But death was not the last chapter in the story of his life. Jesus was raised from the dead, by the power of God. And, because of Jesus, we believe we will live forever with God too.

Hope for the land

It's probably hard to understand this but, the truth is, Simeon couldn't have imagined that salvation would come to him in such a personal way. He was expecting something much different. Simeon's people were anticipating "the consolation of Israel" (2:25) and "the redemption of Jerusalem" (2:38).

The power of God's salvation should shine like a blazing light, for all to see, in our lives and in our life together as Christians.

Israel had long been a nation in trouble. It had been conquered by one foreign power after another. Over the centuries the people of Israel had been oppressed, enslaved, and carried off into exile. In Simeon's time, mighty armies of Rome occupied the cities and the rulers were puppets of the emperor. The people longed to be free. They prayed for a Savior who would feed those who were hungry, right the wrongs that were being done to them, protect those who were powerless, and lead their land into peace. Indeed, God had promised to send just such a Savior.

And, when Simeon saw Jesus, he knew he was seeing that promise fulfilled.

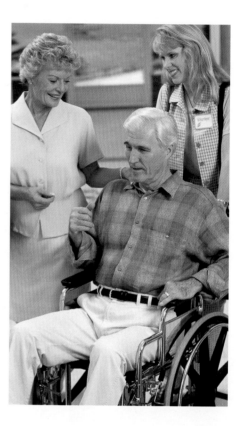

Light for the world

The salvation Simeon saw in the face of Jesus that day in the temple was so much more than he could have imagined. This salvation wasn't just hope for his land; it was hope for his future. It was right here and right now, and it was eternal. It was personal. And it was universal. God's salvation is for the whole world.

"My eyes have seen your salvation," Simeon prayed, "which you have prepared in the presence of all peoples, a light for revelation to the Gentiles" (2:30-32).

God is on a mission to save the whole world. That's why Jesus came. And it is God's intention that, through what Jesus has done for us, *all people* will come to know the saving power of God. The power of God's salvation should shine like a blazing light, for all to see, in our lives and in our life together as Christians. Our lives are like letters upon which God has written a saving message for the world. The people we meet should SEE the difference God's saving love is making in our lives.

Many Christians go to the altar every Sunday morning to receive the gift of saving forgiveness. "This is the body of Christ, given FOR YOU," we are told.

It would be truer if we heard these words: "This is the body of Christ, given for you... *for the sake of the world.*"

What matters to you more at this point in your life—knowing that salvation means you have eternal life or knowing that salvation means Jesus Christ is with you right here, right now?

The Lord's song

When God's hand reaches into the muddy bogs of our daily lives and lifts us out onto dry ground, one thing almost always happens: we sing. When God surprises us with a saving act of grace, we cannot keep from singing.

This is the way it has been since God first gathered the people together and said, "I will take you as my people, and I will be your God" (Exodus 6:7). Pharaoh had enslaved the people of Israel, but God saved them by leading them out of Egypt and freeing them for a new life.

What did the people do when they were set free? They sang. Moses and his sister Miriam led the choir of freed slaves. *Read Exodus 15:1-2, 21* to find out what they sang.

You cannot drive a wedge between the saving and the singing. For that matter, you cannot divide between the saving act and the God who did it. What makes God *God* is that God saves. What makes us sing is that God saves. The song in Exodus 15 even goes so far as to say "The LORD is my strength and my *song*" (15:2 NIV, italics added).

The reason for the singing is that God's salvation affects us in the here and now—not just in some distant, hoped-for tomorrow. In the Old Testa-ment, the word *salvation* refers to God's actions of delivering people right here, right now, in this world. When the Israelites sang, "[God] has become my salvation" (15:2), they meant that God had saved them from Pharaoh.

When we lift our voices today and sing to the living God, we join in saying the same thing. God is active in the world today. God still cares about the daily lives of all people. God wants people to be free today—free politically, free spiritually, free from addiction, free from abuse.

The Lord still reaches into the dark closets of the world and rescues those who have been locked away. God does this for us and calls us to join in this mission.

How can we keep from singing?

When God surprises us with a saving act of grace, we cannot keep from singing.

What would you sing about in a song about God's saving grace? Who needs to hear your "song"?

GROUP TIPS

After you've finished talking about the "Heart of the Matter" article, browse through the rest of the session. Pick one or two additional articles from "Another Look," "Right to the Point," "Bible Basics," or "Right Here, Right Now." Read these articles out loud or silently. Then talk about them. Use the discussion questions to spark your conversation.

You most likely will not get through all of the articles, so pick the ones your group is most interested in. Encourage group members to read the rest of the articles on their own during the week.

ANOTHER LOOK

"Another Look" explores this session's theme from the perspective of another book in the Bible.

Have two people take turns reading Exodus 15:1-2, 21.

Changed lives

Knowing that you're saved leads to a certain settled-ness of spirit, a peace of mind. You don't have to worry and wonder about whether or not you are acceptable to God, or what your final destination will be. But this should never lead to laziness.

Read Luke 19:1-10 for an example of what happens in the life of someone who receives the gift of salvation.

As far as religious people were concerned, Zacchaeus (pronounced Zack-KEE-us) would have been the least likely guy to receive this gift from Jesus. He was a chief tax collector, for one thing, working on behalf of the Roman government that was occupying Israel. What's worse is that he was a Jew working for Rome... and that meant he was a traitor.

Jesus went home with Zacchaeus that day. Salvation came with him... And it changed Zacchaeus forever.

Who knows why Zacchaeus was so desperate to see Jesus that day. And who knows what made Jesus stop to talk to him. Jesus seems to have known Zacchaeus's name. Had they met before? Did someone with Jesus whisper in his ear, to warn him?

"Sir, that man in the tree is a notorious sinner. He is the chief tax collector in town. But don't worry, if he tries anything funny we've got you covered. The only way he'll get close to you is over our dead bodies."

No wonder Jesus stopped. This was *exactly* the kind of person he was looking for. "The Son of Man came to seek out and to save the lost," Jesus reminded everybody (19:10). Jesus went home with Zacchaeus that day. Salvation came with him (19:9). It was unexpected and undeserved. It was here and it was now. And it changed Zacchaeus forever.

"I'm going to fix whatever I've broken," he said. "I am going to right every wrong. I am going to share."

The gift of salvation frees us from worrying about our relationship with God. And that makes it possible for us to attend to our relationships with each other.

How is the gift of salvation changing your life? Where is this gift needed in the world today?

The Old and the New

The Bible has two major sections: the Old Testament, which tells the story of God's mission to and with the people of Israel; and the New Testament, which tells of Christ's mission on behalf of the world.

The two Testaments share many similarities. They both bear witness to the one God who created us and all that exists. They both testify that God has been made known through the history of the chosen people. They both confess that God is active in the world today.

The two Testaments also have some differences. One hurdle for us in reading the Bible is how to deal with the contrasts between the two.

Some of the differences can be explained as developments from an earlier time to a later time. For example, in the Old Testament the people of God are tied closely to the land that God had promised Abraham and Sarah (Genesis 12:1-3). By the time of Jesus, the Israelites had spread far beyond the geographical boundaries of Israel.

Other differences can be explained as changes that resulted from the *incarnation* of God in the person of Jesus. (For more on incarnation, see the "Tip" on this page.) Thus, in the Old Testament, keeping the law is seen as a necessary requirement for belonging to the people. Because of Jesus' death and resurrection, however, the New Testament teaches that keeping the law is not a requirement for belonging (Galatians 2:15-21).

Other differences reflect the changing nature of language and ideas. For example, in the Old Testament *salvation* refers to deliverance from earthly dangers in the here and now. In the New Testament, *salvation* can also mean eternal salvation (John 3:16).

In some cases, people have perceived differences where there are no differences at all! Some people think that the Old Testament is full of judgment while the New Testament is full of grace. This is not true. There is plenty of mercy and grace in the Old Testament—God forgives the people over and over! And the New Testament teaches that Christ will come again to judge all creation.

Keep the Testaments straight and read each one for what it is, remembering the context of when it was written. And, more importantly, remember that both speak of the same God, who created and loves us all.

How will knowing about the similarities and differences between the Old and New Testaments change the way you read the Bible?

GROUP TIPS

RIGHT TO THE POINT

"Right to the Point" goes deeper into this session's theme or explores it from a different angle.

Take turns reading Luke 19:1-10.

BIBLE BASICS

"Bible Basics" will help you learn more about how to read and understand the Bible.

The word *incarnation* means "in the flesh." It is used to describe the Christian truth that in Jesus of Nazareth, God became one of us. That is, in Jesus God meets us flesh to flesh.

Kelly A. Fryer

I told you so

A few years ago, I lost a dear friend to cancer. She had beaten it three times before. She was one of the toughest, most courageous women I have ever known, and one of the kindest and most faithful—an ordinary saint. As I sat and prayed, giving God thanks for her presence in my life, I had a wonderful vision of my friend dancing down the streets of heaven with her Lord. I wrote this song, called "A Golden Crown," in her honor.

Stanza 1:
A cloak of sadness encloses me, as I sit and hold her hand.
I don't know if she can hear me. I don't know if she understands.
My eyes droop closed with weariness. I sit back in my chair.
I remember the way, when I was young, she'd braid bright ribbons in my hair.
Slowly sleep creeps up on me, as if in answer to my prayer.
I drift into an unexpected dream that, on my own, I would never dare.
I see her leaving me; I imagine that she has gone.
And, though the sorrow blinds me, I hear the stir of an unexpected song.

Refrain:
Upon her head he places a golden crown!
He takes her hand and she spins around.
And they are dancing, to the song that he has sung—
    from the beginning of time.
With her name, each word he rhymes.
And they go waltzing, down a street all made of gold,
Like every story she'd ever been told!
And the angels hear me, laughing through my tears.
They can't believe I doubted this...for all those years.
I race to catch her and I'm way too slow.
But, as she swirls away, I swear I can hear her say:
"You see, I told you so."

Stanza 2:
I fight the daylight that pricks my eyes. The last thing I want is to realize—
that it was all a dream—that it wasn't what it seemed.
But, the morning calls, so I stand again and reach out to touch her hand.
I didn't expect it to feel so cold! I didn't know I could feel so old.
She was gone! She was gone.
But, through my sorrow, I heard the stir of an unexpected song. (*refrain*)

© Words by Kelly A. Fryer, 2001; Recorded by Lori Anderson on "Here I Stand," 2004.

What do you picture when you think of heaven? What difference does it make in your life today to know that, one day, you'll end up there?

Wrap up

The gift of salvation is much more than any of us can imagine. It means eternal life. And it means that Jesus Christ is with us, making things right—in our lives and in our world—in the here and now. This gift is personal; it comes to each one of us. And it is universal; it is meant for all people! In fact, God's mission to save the whole world is worked out as people see what has happened in our lives. In some ways, our lives are like windows, through which people can see God's saving power. Through us, God is reaching the world! For next week, read Matthew 4:12-22 and see how God reaches the world through the mission of disciple-making.

What do you hope friends, family, coworkers, and strangers will see when they look at your life this week?

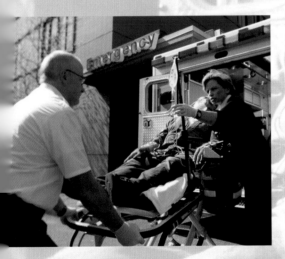

Take turns praying together, out loud. Make it simple. Say thanks for the session. Ask for guidance figuring out what your next steps will be. When everyone has had a turn, pray the Lord's Prayer together out loud:

Our Father in heaven,
Hallowed be your name,
Your kingdom come,
Your will be done,
On earth as in heaven.
Give us today our daily bread.
Forgive us our sins
As we forgive those who sin against us.
Save us from the time of trial
And deliver us from evil.
For the kingdom, the power,
And the glory are yours,
Now and forever. Amen

GROUP TIPS

RIGHT HERE, RIGHT NOW

"Right Here, Right Now" connects this session's theme with real life.

GET GOING

Read "Wrap Up" out loud or silently. Then take turns answering the question.

Decide as a group if you will do any "homework" for the coming week. Consider reading chapter 4 of *No Experience Necessary: Everybody's Welcome*, if you haven't done this already.

Next time you meet will be the end of this unit. You might want to plan a little party to go along with your Bible study time!

Talk about what's next for your group. Will you continue to meet as a group, using Unit Three? Will you split into two groups so you can invite new people to join you? Maybe a few people are feeling called to branch off to start a new group with friends and neighbors who don't have a church home. Some may need a break for awhile. Talk about this! Respect one another and give each other space to wonder out loud about what God is calling you to do.

End by taking turns praying. Be kind and encourage each other.

7 | DISCIPLE-MAKING

God invites us to be part of the mission of disciple-making.

COME AS YOU ARE

God loves us all and wants each of us to be a part of a life-giving relationship with Jesus. In this relationship, we are called disciples. There are no prerequisites for discipleship. There are no IQ or biblical proficiency tests to pass. There is no minimum standard, no background check, no security clearance. Everyone—especially the most unlikely—is invited to follow Jesus into mission. This relationship with Jesus gives us life...true life! And that's why disciples follow Jesus wherever he leads, no matter how scary or dangerous it is. No matter the cost.

Since this is your last session together, you may want to spend time here at the beginning talking about what it has meant to you to be a part of this No Experience Necessary small group. What difference has this experience made? What are the most important things you've learned? Then, if it's still helpful to use a written prayer together, pray this out loud:

Dear God, we give you thanks for your call to follow. Give us courage to answer that call and follow you wherever you lead. In Jesus' name. Amen

JUST 3 QUESTIONS

Open your Bibles to Matthew 4:12-22. Take turns reading this passage, a verse or two at a time, out loud. Then spend some time talking about what is happening in this passage, including what you are hearing God say here. Use these three questions as a starting point to have this conversation:

1 | **What do you think God is doing here?**

2 | **What do you hear God saying to you, personally?**

3 | **What do you hear God saying to us (as a small group, congregation, community, nation)?**

GROUP TIPS

COME AS YOU ARE

Group members may be feeling and thinking all kinds of things in this final session of Unit Two. Some may be surprised they made it all the way through! Others, for whom this has been a struggle, may be relieved. Still others may be sad that this unit is about to end. Give each other space during this check-in time. God has been at work—and that doesn't look the same for everybody! Listen to one another and honor the unique experience each has had.

JUST 3 QUESTIONS

This should be old hat now. Have the group consider using these three questions to think not just about the Bible, but about every experience. God can speak to us in all kinds of ways. As you listen to a sermon, watch a movie, have a conversation with a friend, read a book—whatever!—ask yourself, "What is God doing here? What do I hear God saying to me here?" Tune in to God's voice speaking to you in your daily life. Listening for God shouldn't end here.

A weird plan

Jesus burst onto the scene with a radical message: God's kingdom is coming. And it is here! This meant, of course, that a new king was in town...a very unusual king. This new king would not rule by force. He would not put his own needs and concerns above those of his subjects. He would be gentle and giving. He would lift up the lowly and humble the proud. He would forgive the sinful and seek out the lost. He would be willing, even, to sacrifice his own life for the sake of his people. This king, of course, was Jesus himself. (You can read what Jesus said about this new kingdom in Matthew 5–7; 13; 18–20.)

> "Come and be a part of what I'm doing!" Jesus invited. "Come learn to fish for people with me!"

A motley crew

The first thing Jesus did, once the public phase of his ministry began, was to gather some followers. He wasn't very choosy about who these people were. They came, for the most part, from the lowest strata of society: people in the working class and the rural poor, and those who were outcast because of illness or lifestyle or unfortunate circumstances. They were, in the eyes of their world, nobodies. Jesus made them somebodies.

He made them disciples.

No wonder, then, when Jesus said "Follow me" to those fishers on the beach that day, they dropped what they were doing to answer his call. "Come and be a part of what I'm doing!" Jesus invited. "Come learn to fish for people with me!" They didn't even hesitate.

"We're right behind you, Jesus," they said.

They had to have known they'd never get a better offer. They had to have sensed, somehow, that Jesus was about to lead them on the adventure of a lifetime. They had to figure that, if they ever wanted to have their lives really MEAN something, now was their chance.

This relationship ...turns us, sometimes to our surprise, into fishers for people.

To be sure, these people (and all the others who followed) would mess things up along the way. They would misunderstand Jesus' message and chicken out when things got tough and, when he needed them most, at least one of them would deny even knowing him. But, for some weird reason, God's mission— of loving and saving and reconciling and re-creating the whole world— includes inviting the most unlikely people to be a part of making it happen. It has always been that way. That's how it works today.

An irresistible relationship

There is something irresistible about the relationship Jesus invites us to be a part of that draws us in. This is the same kind of relationship that exists between the Father and the Son and the Holy Spirit, with a mutual respect and a love that goes beyond words. There is a willingness to give everything for the sake of the other, to do even the hardest things, to take even the most dangerous journeys.

This relationship begins with a simple invitation that comes out of the blue.

We don't deserve it. Maybe we weren't even looking for it. We were busy washing our cars or our nets when it came.

For no good reason that we can think of, Jesus says, "Come be my disciple," and what he means is, "Come be a part of this thing that my Father and I are up to."

This relationship changes everything. It helps us see ourselves the way we really are, the way we have been created to be. It gives us courage to try new things and tackle huge challenges. It melts our hearts and makes us want to share what we have been given with everyone. It turns us, sometimes to our surprise, into fishers for people.

"Come on, everybody!" we say to our family and friends and even strangers on the street. "There is somebody I want you to meet."

Maybe this isn't such a strange plan, after all.

What was it like for you to be invited to follow Jesus? When did it happen? Through whom did you hear the invitation?

A strange message

When Paul went to the city of Corinth to make disciples there, he brought a strange message. According to him, "I decided to know nothing among you except Jesus Christ, and him crucified" (1 Corinthians 2:2).

What was strange about this? Well, crosses were not pleasant things. A cross was *a means of torturing someone to death*! And Paul's message was this: "If you want to know what God is like, you have to look at Jesus as he was tortured to death on the cross. That is what God is like! God is a Lord who is willing to be tortured to death for you."

> **God is a Lord who is willing to be tortured to death for you.**

Crazy message, right? Paul admitted as much when he wrote that the world sees the message of the cross as "foolishness" (1:18). Many who heard Paul thought so too. Some graffiti uncovered in ancient Rome shows a person worshiping an ass who has been crucified. The writing beneath it quips, "Alexamenos worships his God."

The objection is obvious: Why should we be disciples of a God who dies, and dies in such a pathetic way? The only answer is: because this is what God is truly like.

People would prefer that we tell them that God wants them to be rich. People would prefer that we tell them that if they become a Christian, all their troubles will disappear and they will waltz down Easy Street for the rest of their lives. People would prefer that we tell them if they follow a set of Commandments, then God will bless them.

So if people would prefer this, why don't we give them what they want? Because it is not true.

We are called to make disciples of *the crucified one,* Jesus Christ, who said, "Take up the cross and follow me" (Matthew 10:38), the same Jesus Christ who refused to fight back when he was being tortured and killed, even though the heavenly Father had given all power on earth to him.

One of the things this means is that when we make disciples, the cross is what we must proclaim and the cross is what people must follow. As Paul said, this message is foolishness to some, but to those being saved it is "the power of God" (1 Corinthians 1:18).

In what ways can you and the church be involved in making disciples who follow the crucified one?

After you've finished talking about the "Heart of the Matter" article, browse through the rest of the session. Pick one or two additional articles from "Another Look," "Right to the Point," "Bible Basics," or "Right Here, Right Now." Read these articles out loud or silently. Then talk about them. Use the discussion questions to spark your conversation.

You most likely will not get through all of the articles, so pick the ones your group is most interested in. Encourage group members to read the rest of the articles on their own during the week.

ANOTHER LOOK

"Another Look" explores this session's theme from the perspective of another book in the Bible.

The cost of discipleship

Those fishermen immediately left their nets and followed Jesus. Somehow they must have known they would never have a better offer. A life with Jesus is a life that matters. But that doesn't mean it's easy.

Read Matthew 10:34-39 and count the cost of discipleship.

> The point is that following Jesus means following him *wherever* he leads you. That means putting what Jesus wants ahead of what you want, every time.

For the earliest Christians, the reality was that following Jesus often meant cutting family ties. Sometimes it meant facing arrest and even death. These things still happen in various places around the globe today.

In our culture, usually the worst thing that happens to people who answer Jesus' call is that their friends and family give them funny looks. But sometimes, even here, following Jesus can lead to big trouble.

Some of Jesus' followers today are risking their lives by working in the scariest neighborhoods, trying to bring hope and peace in the midst of poverty and gang warfare. Others are risking their reputations and livelihoods by blowing the whistle on unethical behavior. Still others are pouring their time and their money into efforts to eradicate illiteracy, end hunger, preserve the environment, and grant equal rights to all people: in the workplace, in our churches, in our nation, and across the world.

The point is that following Jesus means following him *wherever* he leads you. That means putting what Jesus wants ahead of what you want, every time. It means putting Jesus and his work ahead of your own desires. It means that his agenda comes first in your life.

When Jesus says "take up the cross" (10:38), sometimes he means it literally. People have died for their faith. But it is also an image of the kind of life that is required of every disciple.

Why does anyone do it?

Well, Jesus describes this very strange paradox. (A *paradox* is a situation where two or more ideas appear to be true but also appear to contradict each other.) He says the only way to find *true* life is to give your life away. In fact, he says, if you try to *hang on* to your life (including your agenda, your time, your stuff, etc.), you're going to be sure to lose it all in the end.

Those fishermen were never going to get a better offer. They were never going to get a scarier one, either.

Describe a time when you felt like you were really living...because you were giving yourself away.

Not a self-improvement project

Martin Luther, one of the men who helped start the Reformation of the Christian church in the 1500s, taught that to be a true disciple a person must be a follower of the *cross* and not a follower of his or her own desire for *glory*.

The point is that many of us who try to follow Jesus are really only using the faith as a costume we put on in order to try to chase after our own spiritual wishes.

> The cross says: Nothing you can do is able to add to what Jesus did for you on the cross.

To put this another way, many of us *use God* and God's commandments as a sort of "spiritual self-improvement project." We sometimes use the faith as an excuse to try to author our own spiritual achievements. We try to save ourselves, rather than truly follow Jesus. At times we attempt to prove that we are worthy, rather than accept Christ's free love and grace.

There is a lesson for those who will read the Bible, who will be disciples of Jesus, and who will join in making disciples. That lesson is this: This is God's gig. God is the one who is doing the miracles, making disciples, and changing lives.

We are just followers. And often not very good followers, at that!

The cross is so important for disciples because it reminds us that this is God's gig. The cross says: Nothing you can do is able to add to what Jesus did for you on the cross. The cross says: We didn't die or even help Jesus die, Jesus died all by himself—and he is still the one doing things today.

The cross reminds us that it doesn't matter how well we pray, it only matters that a loving God hears our prayers. The cross reminds us that it doesn't matter how perfectly we sing in worship, it only matters that the Spirit of God is there with us in worship.

As you read the Bible, *always look for what God is doing*! This is about God's actions—God's love, mercy, and command—this is God's gig.

What's your reaction to the statement, "This is God's gig"? What things remind you that it's what God does that is important?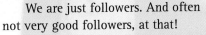

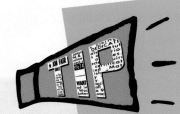

According to Matthew and Mark, the first thing Jesus did after being tempted in the wilderness was to call disciples to follow him (Matthew 4:18-22; Mark 1:16-20). This suggests that following Jesus is central to God's mission in the world.

GROUP TIPS

RIGHT TO THE POINT

"Right to the Point" goes deeper into this session's theme or explores it from a different angle.

Take turns reading Matthew 10:34-39.

BIBLE BASICS

"Bible Basics" will help you learn more about how to read and understand the Bible.

Kelly A. Fryer

The world needs what we have

Not long ago, I received an e-mail message from a man who lives across the country from me. He is a security guard who works in a medical setting. He's also a member of his congregation's council. He told me that when the tsunami hit Southeast Asia in 2004, tragically killing so many people and forcing even more into homelessness, he was asked by a group of doctors to take medical supplies to the scene of the devastation. He didn't want to do this—and he wasn't ashamed to admit it. Doing it would require an enormous sacrifice. It would take him away from home and family, for no one could say how long. It would take his precious vacation and personal time. Most frightening of all, this trip would put him in jeopardy, even life-threatening danger. The costs, in many ways, seemed too high.

But he and the other members of the church council were in the final chapters of a book study. And one night, in the midst of his decision-making process, it was his turn to lead. The chapter for that night was titled "The World Needs What We Have." And this chapter says, "The church may be the only organization on the planet that exists entirely for the sake of those people who don't belong to it yet. In fact, as soon as we forget this and start making it all about ourselves, we stop being the church" (Kelly A. Fryer, *Reclaiming the "L" Word:*

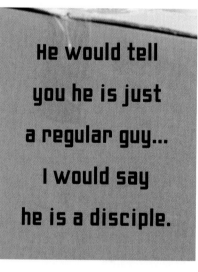

He would tell you he is just a regular guy... I would say he is a disciple.

Renewing the Church from its Lutheran Core, Augsburg Fortress, 2003, page 87). During the conversation at church that night, things became clear. "I know what I have to do," my new friend said to his brothers and sisters around the table. And they knew he was right.

This brave man took those supplies into the heart of the destruction. Who knows how many lives he saved! After what seemed like an eternity he made it back safely to his family, but he tells me that he has not been the same. His heart is softer. His faith is stronger. His testimony is more confident; in fact, it is changing his church, as well.

He would tell you he is just a regular guy, who did what he thought he had to do. I would say he is a disciple.

I think Jesus would say that too.

What is the scariest thing you have ever done because you knew it was what God wanted you to do?

Wrap up

God is madly in love with this world and everyone in it! God wants to make things right—reconciling, re-creating, and saving us. God wants to be in a relationship with each one of us that gives us an opportunity to really make a difference. God wants us to have *true* life. That's why Jesus calls us to be his disciples, to follow wherever he leads. This will be scary sometimes, and hard. Those who answer the call end up carrying a cross. But there is joy on this path, and hope and peace and life. That's why those fishermen immediately dropped their nets and left everything to go with Jesus. They knew a better offer would never come along.

What is God asking you to "drop" right now in order to follow Jesus? What is holding you back?

Take turns praying before you go. When everyone has had a turn, pray the Lord's Prayer together out loud:

**Our Father in heaven,
Hallowed be your name,
Your kingdom come,
Your will be done,
On earth as in heaven.
Give us today our daily bread.
Forgive us our sins
As we forgive those who sin against us.
Save us from the time of trial
And deliver us from evil.
For the kingdom, the power,
And the glory are yours,
Now and forever. Amen**

GROUP TIPS

RIGHT HERE, RIGHT NOW

"Right Here, Right Now" connects this session's theme with real life.

GET GOING

Read "Wrap Up" out loud or silently. Then take turns answering the questions.

This is the last session in Unit Two, so spend some time talking about what's next. Some of you may want to continue meeting as a No Experience Necessary group, using Unit Three. Who else can you invite to join you next time? Others may want to start a new group of their own so that they can invite ALL new people. A few may decide to take a break for awhile. Give group members space to do what they believe God is calling them to do. Encourage one another, whatever the next steps look like!

End by praying together. Hopefully, by now, most of your group has become comfortable praying out loud. Go around the circle and give each person a chance to pray and thank God for something she or he has gotten out of this group.

Best, Ernest. *Second Corinthians (Interpretation: A Bible Commentary for Teaching and Preaching)*. Louisville, Kentucky: Westminster John Knox Press, 1987.

Bliese, Richard H. and Craig Van Gelder, editors. *The Evangelizing Church: A Lutheran Contribution*. Minneapolis: Augsburg Fortress, 2005.

Cousar, Charles B. *Galatians (Interpretation: A Bible Commentary for Teaching and Preaching)*. Louisville, Kentucky: Westminster John Knox Press, 1986.

Craddock, Fred B. *Luke (Interpretation: A Bible Commentary for Teaching and Preaching)*. Louisville, Kentucky: Westminster John Knox Press, 1990.

González, Justo L. *Acts: The Gospel of the Spirit*. Maryknoll, New York: Orbis Books, 2001.

Guder, Darrell L. *The Continuing Conversion of the Church*. Grand Rapids, Michigan: William B. Eerdmans, 2000.

Hutton, Rodney R. *Fortress Introduction to the Prophets*. Minneapolis: Fortress, 2004.

Kirk, J. Andrew. *What Is Mission? Theological Explorations*. Minneapolis: Fortress Press, 2000.

Koester, Craig R. *Symbolism in the Fourth Gospel: Meaning, Mystery, Community* second edition. Minneapolis: Augsburg Fortress, 2003.

Limburg, James. *Hosea-Micah (Interpretation: A Bible Commentary for Teaching and Preaching)*. Louisville, Kentucky: Westminster John Knox Press, 1988.

Meeks, Wayne, editor. *The HarperCollins Study Bible: New Revised Standard Version*. New York: HarperSanFrancisco, 1993.

Metzger, Bruce M. and Michael Coogan, editors. *The Oxford Guide to People & Places of the Bible*. New York: Oxford University Press, 2001.

Nissen, Johannes. *New Testament and Mission: Historical and Hermeneutical Perspectives*. Frankfurt am Main: Peter Lang Publishing, 1999.

Nolland, John. *Word Biblical Commentary 35A: Luke 1–9:20*. Dallas: Word, Incorporated, 1989.

Powell, Mark Allan. *Fortress Introduction to the Gospels*. Minneapolis: Fortress, 1998.

Rhoads, David. *The Challenge of Diversity: The Witness of Paul and the Gospels*. Minneapolis: Fortress, 1996.

Rhoads, David, Joanna Dewey, and Donald Michie. *Mark as Story: An Introduction to the Narrative of a Gospel* second edition. Minneapolis: Fortress, 1999.

Stumme, Wayne (editor). *Bible and Mission*. Minneapolis: Augsburg, 1986; out of print.

Williamson, Lamar, Jr. *Mark (Interpretation: A Bible Commentary for Teaching and Preaching)*. Louisville, Kentucky: Westminster John Knox Press, 1983.

Willimon, William H. *Acts (Interpretation: A Bible Commentary for Teaching and Preaching)*. Louisville, Kentucky: Westminster John Knox Press, 1988.